ENGLISH FOR ACADEMIC PURPOS

General Editor: Vaughan James

BUSINESS STUDIES

C. V. James

Cassell

Cassell Publishers Ltd
Artillery House
Artillery Row
London
SW1P 1RT

© Cassell Publishers Limited 1989

All rights reserved. This book is protected by copyright. No part of it may be reproduced, stored in a retrieval system, or transmitted in any form or by any means, electronic, mechanical, photocopying, recording or otherwise, without prior permission from the Publishers.

First published in 1989

British Library Cataloguing in Publication Data

James, C. Vaughan (Caradog Vaughan), *1925–*
   Business studies.
   Student's book
   1. Business studies
   I. Title
   658

ISBN 0 304 31593 1

A series designed and developed by Passim Ltd, Oxford, and Associates

Printed in England

Business Studies Teacher's Book 0 304 31594 X
Cassettes 0 304 31595 8

CONTENTS

UNIT

1.	Starting a Business	1
2.	The Problem of Cash Flow (1)	7
3.	The Problem of Cash Flow (2)	15
4.	The Paper Chase	24
5.	Lies and Statistics	33
	Check Your Progress (1)	44
6.	Dealing with People (1)	48
7.	Dealing with People (2)	59
8.	Managing the Paperwork	69
9.	Illustrating the Point	80
10.	Catching the Eye	91
	Check Your Progress (2)	101
11.	It Pays to Advertise	105
12.	Planning the Attack	114
13.	Using Computers (1)	121
14.	Using Computers (2)	131
15.	The Six Ways of Improving Profits	142

INTRODUCTION

This course has three purposes. It is intended:
- to introduce you to the **contents** of Business Studies;
- to provide examples of authentic texts written in the **language** typical of the subject;
- to help you to practise the **skills** you will need in order to study the subject via English and to use it when you have learned it

No knowledge of Business Studies is assumed, but if you work through the book carefully you will certainly learn a great deal about it. We do not set out to give comprehensive coverage, but the material does embrace most of the basic concepts. In this sense it is a basic textbook of Business Studies.

All the texts are taken from publications about Business Studies. They are not simplified for learners of English: the language you will encounter in them is exactly what you will meet in real life. We assume that you will have already taken a course of general English and are familiar with the main grammatical structures and much of the vocabulary of everyday use. There may be no such thing as Business Studies English, but there are a number of words and expressions commonly used in Business Studies contexts and there are a number of structures also in common use, and these have been isolated for you to practise. So in this sense, this is a textbook of English.

The most important aim of the course, however, is to help you to acquire and develop the skills you will need in order to learn your subject and, when you have finished the course, to use what you will have learned.

When you begin to study a new subject, you do so in two main ways: by **reading** and by **listening**. These are the major means of access to new knowledge and it is on these that we concentrate, via the **book** — for reading, and the **tapes** — for listening. In order to attack all these aims, we have divided each of the 15 units into 8 sections, closely related but each with a slightly different emphasis. Below we give a brief description of each section, so that at any point in any unit you will know exactly what you are expected to do and why you are doing it. The pattern is the same for all units.

A. UNDERSTANDING A PRINTED TEXT (1): In this section you are given a passage to read, usually including a diagram or table, to introduce the topic of the unit. You should first read it through, even if you do not understand it all, looking especially at the way it is set out in paragraphs, with side headings, marginal notes, captions, etc. This will give you a general idea of what it is about and how it is arranged. To help you to identify the most important points in the reading passage, a small number of questions are given, the answers to which you can look out for as you read. You will probably need to read it several times.

B. CHECK YOUR UNDERSTANDING: When you are clear about the general meaning of the passage, you can work through it in more detail with your dictionary. In this section you will be asked to answer a number of detailed questions. You could tackle them by jotting down a few notes and then turning your notes into complete answers, which your teacher will check. You should *always* have a dictionary handy and *never* be too proud (or too lazy!) to look things up.

C. INCREASE YOUR VOCABULARY: In this section you are asked to look at certain words which are used in the text, and there are several kinds of activity to help you remember them. Notice that they are not all new or technical terms; it is often familiar words used in an unfamiliar way that will cause you trouble.

D. CHECK YOUR GRAMMAR: There are probably no new grammatical structures in the texts, but you may need reminding of some of them. The most important ones arising from the texts are revised and practised in this section.

E. UNDERSTANDING A LECTURE / H. UNDERSTANDING DISCOURSE: Sections A–D are all concerned with gaining access to new information through reading, but an important source of information is through listening — to lectures, talks, discussions, even simple conversations between fellow students — so sections E and H are both based on the recordings, to which you should listen (usually several times) before attempting to answer the questions or perform the activities given in your book. You will hear a variety of voices and accents, all speaking at the sort of speed that is customary in an English-speaking environment.

F. UNDERSTANDING A PRINTED TEXT (2) / G. CHECK YOUR UNDERSTANDING: These two sections are very similar to A and B, but the questions in section G are presented in several different ways.

Although we hope that you will enjoy working through this course, we do not expect you to find it easy. At various times you will probably start wondering how much you have been learning — or your teacher will want to find out what progress you are making. So after Units 5 and 10 we have included progress checks (not tests!) so that you can get a fairly clear idea of this. By the time you have completed Unit 15, you will be ready for anything!

Some of the texts are written in American English, which has some differences from British English, especially in spelling (e.g. *Br.* vapour, *Am.* vapor). You might find it useful to keep a running list of such examples. Remember that they are equally acceptable, but you should avoid mixing them in a single piece of writing.

Vaughan James   Oxford, 1989

STARTING A BUSINESS

UNIT 1

A. Understanding a printed text (1)

The following text introduces some of the problems — especially **financial** — which arise when a new business is to be started. Look at the way the passage is constructed, with different paragraphs dealing with specific aspects. Pay attention to the side-headings and to the diagram and caption.

Now look at the following questions and read the passage through quickly to find the answers. Remember that you do not need to understand every word in order to answer the questions.

1. What is the passage about?
2. What is the first thing you need if you want to start a business?
3. Why is it good to start production as soon as possible?
4. What does Figure 1 show?

THE FLOW OF FUNDS

The object of running any business is to make money, and the first requirement in order to start up a new business is, likewise, money. It does not necessarily have to be a very large amount — it depends on the business — and there are lots of encouraging stories of entrepreneurs making vast fortunes out of very small initial funds. But however much it is, it has to be managed well if the business is to survive and prosper. Perhaps a more reliable guide is the old saying that 'money breeds money'.

In this unit we shall look first at how money flows through a small manufacturing business, rather like water flowing through a circulation system. This is illustrated in Figure 1.

Introduction

1   If a business is to be started, funds must first be obtained from some source. The money may come from the would-be businessman's personal savings — in which case it is called *equity capital* — or it may be borrowed from a bank. *Loans* to be repaid over a period of one to four years are short-term loans; loans for a period of five years or more are long-term. Whatever the source, the money has to be obtained and, when it has been obtained, it must be properly handled.

The first requirements in starting a new business

When a business has been formed, a number of important decisions will have to be made, such as what premises are to be used and, for a manufacturing concern, what plant and machinery will be needed. Such items are known as *fixed assets* and require a heavy outlay of money. Then a supplier has to be found, from whom the materials needed for manufacturing the product — the *raw materials* — will be obtained, and the *terms of credit* will have to be agreed. Then there are a number of other decisions to be made, such as how many people are to be employed and what equipment they will need, how many telephones are to be installed, etc. And all of these will require financing.

The need for decisions

2   Once these decisions have been made, it will be necessary to implement them and start the manufacturing process as soon as possible. Until the business has a product for which there is a demand, and has succeeded in selling that product, there will be a continuous drain from the pool of money. If the business finances are not properly managed, it may well disappear altogether. The 'pumps' in Figure 1 represent the points at which good management can speed up the whole process. The successful integration of people and materials requires good management, and the more effectively this is done, the better for the business.

Starting production

1

Controlling stock

Balancing stock and work in progress (WIP)

3   There is always a leak of resources through the tap at the pool of stock (Tap 1). This is a controllable leak and its size depends upon the success or otherwise with which the raw materials are managed. If store facilities are poor, and the storeman is not very interested in his job, the leak will be large. The loss can be minimised by a good system of stores control backed by well trained staff.

4   During and immediately following the production process, there are two other 'pools' in which the resources employed in a business become trapped. These are *work in progress* (WIP) and *finished stock*. In even the most successfully managed businesses there will be, at the end of each accounting period, some items that are between the raw material and finished goods stage. Management would like all items to be produced as quickly as possible but, as things take time to make, work in progress can never be eliminated. It should not, however, be allowed to build up to an unnecessarily high level. There are problems, too, in deciding how work in progress should be valued, and the system necessary to keep track of it has to be specified. Finished stock should be sold and delivered as quickly as possible, although in some cases — where the demand for the goods is seasonal — it may be necessary to have facilities to hold quite a lot of finished stock. Toy manufacture, where the bulk of the sales takes place at Christmas, is one example of this. The loss of resources at the finished stock stage can be serious unless a good system of stores control is employed. The loss can be due to pilfering, breakages and general deterioration. Stock levels in the UK used to be much higher in the manufacturing sector than in America, Germany and Japan, but the destocking brought about by recession lowered them.

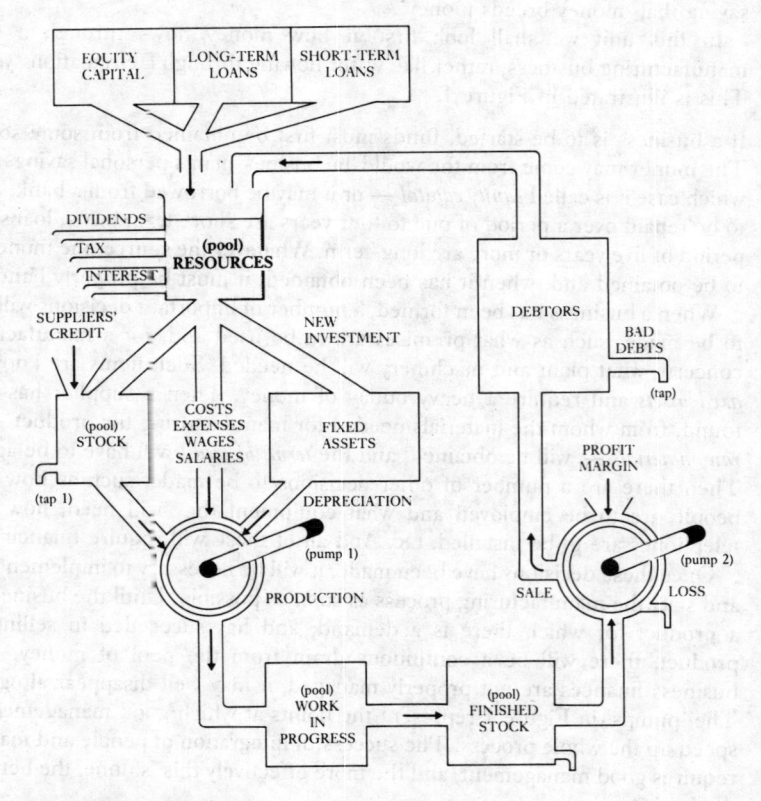

Figure 1 Business Funds Flow

B. Check your understanding

1. Now read the text carefully, looking up anything you do not understand, and answer the following questions:

1. What is the object of running a business?
2. What is the first thing you need if you want to start up a new business?
3. What are personal savings invested in starting a business called?
4. What alternative sources of funds might be used?
5. What is long-term loan?
6. What kinds of fixed assets can you name?
7. What do you call the materials from which the product is to be made?
8. Why should the manufacturing process be started as soon as possible?
9. What determines the size of leak from the pool of stock?
10. What may happen if storage facilities are poor?
11. How can the resulting loss be minimised?
12. In what other 'pools' may business resources be trapped?
13. In general, should the amount of work in progress be kept high or low?
14. In what circumstances should large stocks be built up?
15. What was the cause of destocking in the United Kingdom and many other countries in recent years?

2. Look at Figure 1 and answer the following questions:

1. What are the main inputs of funds?
2. What expenditures have to be met from the pool of resources?
3. What payments have to be made in addition to costs?
4. What additional input enables you to acquire stock?
5. What would be the effect of slowing down at pump 1?

C. Increase your vocabulary

Explain in your own words the meaning of the following words and expressions as used in the text:
- Introduction, line 4: entrepreneurs
  - 7: 'money breeds money'
- paragraph 1, line 3: equity capital
  - 4: short-term loan
  - 5: long-term loan

- paragraph 1, line 9: plant and machinery
  - 10: fixed assets
  - 10: heavy outlay

- paragraph 3, line 1: leak of resources
  - 2: controllable leak
  - 4–5: the loss can be minimised

- paragraph 4, line 4: accounting period
  - 11–12: the demand for the goods is seasonal
  - 13: finished stock
  - 16: general deterioration

D. Check your grammar

Remember?
The nature of the business *will already have been decided.*
You will already have decided the nature of the business.

cf: However much it is, it has to be managed well. (indirect/impersonal)
However much it is, you have to manage it well. (direct/personal)
The first example is not addressed at anyone in particular; it is an impersonal statement. The second example is directed at you, the reader, personally. The difference is not one of meaning but one of style.

Now make the alternative forms of the following (taken from the text) and explain the difference:
1. If a business is to be started, funds must first be obtained.
2. It may be borrowed from a bank.
3. When it has been obtained, it must be properly handled.
4. When a business has been formed, a number of decisions will have to be made.
5. All of these will require financing.

Can you find other examples in the text and explain them?

E. Understanding a lecture

Listen to the lecture given on your tape. It is split into sections to make it easier to understand. Then look at the questions given below and listen again for the answers. You may find it useful to stop after every section and perhaps repeat it. Answer the questions in your own words:

1. What are the three general reasons for failure cited by the lecturer?

2. Which does he think is the most important?

3. What does he say is the most important aspect of management?

4. What are the five lessons he draws from examples of bad management?

5. What does he give as the golden rule?

F. Understanding a printed text (2)

STARTING TO TRADE

1   The next point at which good management can greatly improve the resources available to the business is by selling and distributing the finished goods as quickly as possible and obtaining the money from the firm's customers in the shortest possible time. There is a loss at the time of sale, which good procedures can largely eliminate, caused by damage, pilferage and below-standard items that are returned, as well as by items incorrectly delivered. It is here that the greatest potential loss occurs, that of bad debts — people who take delivery of goods but do not pay for them. Most business is conducted on credit, and, with the difficulty in obtaining sales, credit has become easier to obtain. It is one element in the marketing mix and its terms depend on many things, including the custom and practice of the trade, and the pressures on the company to make a sale. Nearly all businesses suffer from bad debts, and, in order to keep them to a minimum, an efficient system of credit control is essential. The practice of *factoring* your debts, which entails employing a third person who obtains your money for you for a fee, is widespread in America and growing elsewhere. It has the advantage of giving the business money to use more quickly than would otherwise be the case. The criticism most usually levied against it is that it destroys the special relationship between the organization and its customers.

Credit

2   The money collected from the customers now replaces some of that used in starting the business, but the 'taps' of dividends, tax and interest have to be considered. Shareholders' dividends can be paid only out of profits, so if no profits have been made no dividends will be expected. If profits have been made, dividends may be paid at the discretion of the owners, but this is not a requirement. If a business is continually making a profit but refuses to pay dividends, without good reason, it will find it difficult to obtain money from the public when it next needs it. Interest has to be paid whether the business is profitable or not, which means that businesses have to ensure that they do not borrow so much that they cannot afford the interest charges. The amount of interest to be paid depends on the size and terms of borrowing, which good management can ensure remain within the capability of the business. Tax is chargeable on profits but is at a minimum in the early years of manufacturing businesses, because of capital allowances, as well as when any large capital investment programme has been undertaken.

Dividends, tax and interest

3   The amount of money that a business has at its disposal to enable it to operate until more money has been received is called its working capital, the difference between the capital it will have available within the next four or five months and what it will have to pay within the same period. It may need enough working capital to keep it going for five months before it receives any further resources.

Working capital

This may be broken down as:

Obtaining raw materials	4 weeks	
Manufacturing process	4 weeks	
Held in stock	4 weeks	These periods are for example only and will vary from industry to industry
Collect money from customer	8 weeks	
Total	20 weeks	

All this time the costs, expenses, wages and salaries have to be met. It is for this reason that it is important to ensure that the working capital and other financial resources of the business are properly managed.

G. Check your understanding

1. Read through the text very carefully, looking up anything you do not understand. Then answer the following questions:
- What is the benefit of selling the product as soon as possible?
- What is the purpose of credit control?
- What is the disadvantage of factoring debts?
- Does a profitable business *have* to pay dividends?
- What is meant by working capital?

2. Say whether the following statements are true or false:
- When it is difficult to get sales, it is also difficult to get credit. ☐
- Getting someone else to collect the money owed to you improves your relationship with your customers. ☐
- Profitable businesses do not have to pay dividends to their shareholders. ☐
- If a business is not profitable, it does not have to pay interest on the money it has borrowed. ☐
- The tax charged on profits is greater in the first few years after a business is started. ☐

H. Understanding discourse

Listen to the recording on your tape of a talk given by the Managing Director of a company. Play it right through in order to get a general idea of what it contains. Then look at the questions below and at the scheme of the organisation of a company. Then play the tape again, section by section, and make notes for your answers to the questions. When you have done this, expand your answers into complete sentences and enter the titles of the departmental managers in the appropriate place in the scheme. (You will add to this for the next three units, until it is complete.)

1. Are all companies organised in the same way?
2. Why is it sometimes necessary to change the organisation?
3. Who appoints the Chairman?
4. What is his function?
5. What are the duties of the Managing Director?

Now list the six departmental managers and enter them on the scheme below.

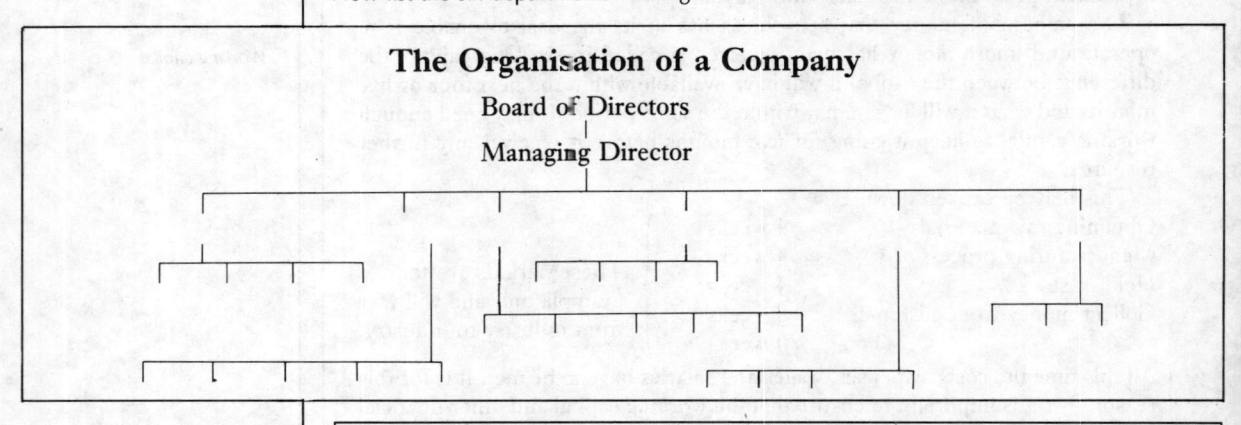

The Organisation of a Company

Board of Directors
|
Managing Director

Reading passages (1) and (2) were taken, amended, from: David Davies, *The Art of Managing Finance*, McGraw-Hill (UK), 1985.

THE PROBLEM OF CASH FLOW (1)

UNIT 2

A. Understanding a printed text (1)

The following passage introduces the topic of **the management of cash resources** in a business, the problem of cash flow. Look at the way the passage is constructed, with paragraphs dealing with different aspects. Pay special attention to the side-headings, the illustrations and the captions.

Now look at the following questions and read through the passage quickly to find the answers. Remember, you do not have to understand every word in the passage in order to answer the questions.

1. What, in your own words, is the passage about?
2. What main form of cash does it deal with?
3. What does Figure 11.1 show?
4. What is the point of Table 11.1?

MANAGING THE CASH

1 More businesses fail for lack of cash than for any other factor, and while profits are important because in the longer term they generate cash, it is the management of cash resources in the business that is of prime importance.

Why businesses fail

Without cash a company cannot:

The uses of cash

– Pay creditors.
– Pay wages and salaries.
– Invest in stocks of materials, parts, and finished products.
– Invest in the future.
– Design and develop new products or services.

2 The major flows of cash income are:

Major cash flow of income

1. Cash arising from sales revenue (invoiced goods).
2. Cash arising from the sale of current assets—unwanted finished stocks, materials, and parts stocks.
3. Cash arising from the sale of fixed assets, i.e., from liquidating the capital resources of a business. This is good when the assets are unused, but not if the assets may be necessary for future business.

Other forms of cash income are:

4. Loans, mortgages, overdrafts, share or stock issues.

These have to be paid back, and usually at some interest or cost of capital.

Working capital

3   In this section we will deal mainly with the forms of cash that can be released most easily, namely, working capital. Figure 11.1 shows typical cash flow periods for some UK companies.

An example of the working capital cycle for a five-year period is given in

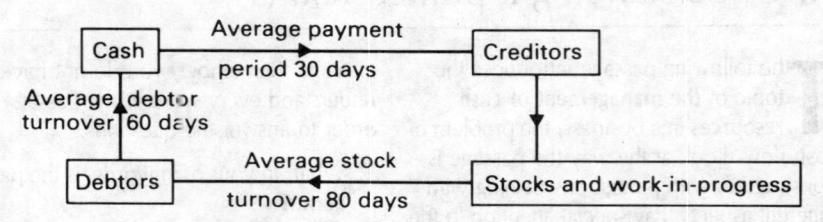

Fig. 11.1   Typical cash flow periods for some UK companies

Table 11.1. It can be seen just how rapidly the working capital needs have expanded during that time. The question then arises: have these increased in proportion to sales or as a result of poor cash flow management? The ratio of working capital needs to sales can be seen by the number of days required for total working capital: this has generally risen, largely because of the increase in the average stock turnover, which has increased from 50 to 80 days. Stock turnover improvement is necessary.

Effective cash management

4   Effective cash management usually means control over two main factors:

1. *Control of debtors.* Standards should be set for the typical payment periods normally expected for the country in question. In some countries no debtors are allowed: invoices are sent to the customer and their banks and the amount is credited immediately. Other countries may have laws about the number of days over which debts are allowed.

Debtors

If there is no legal stipulation, then an analysis of debtor payment times (an 'age analysis') is needed, and those customers in arrears need chasing in order to get payments.

Alternative arrangements may also be applicable for those who persistently take too much credit, e.g., requiring cash in advance or on delivery, bankers' drafts, export credit guarantees, etc. Some companies rely on 'factors' to pay them the cash for invoiced goods... ... ...
... ...   The factors are responsible for the collection of debts, but this is always at a high cost to the company.

Table 11.1   Example of a working capital cycle for a five-year period

Year	Average stock turnover £'000	days	Average debtor turnover £'000	days	Average payment period £'000	days	Total working capital needs £'000	days
1	150	50	100	60	80	30	170	80
2	250	60	120	65	100	35	270	90
3	400	65	180	55	160	40	420	80
4	600	70	240	55	200	35	640	90
5	900	80	80	60	250	30	950	110

2. *Control over stocks and work in progress.* More precise means of managing and controlling stocks and work in progress in companies is generally essential. This is achieved by:

   (a) Using the 80/20 rule, in which 20 per cent of the products give rise to 80 per cent of the value. The planning, scheduling and control of the 20 per cent needs detailed attention compared to the 80 per cent of the products that provide only 20 per cent of the value.

   (b) Using material requirement planning and/or scientific stock control methods for controlling the purchase and use of materials.

   (c) Using modern production control methods of planning factory activities. This may involve the methods given in (a) and (b) above, plus planning and controlling the capacity of both people and machines so as to ensure good material flows, uninterrupted supplies, and the reduction of delays on the shop-floor.

Stocks and WIP

5 A good cash flow constitutes the life-blood of a business; therefore it has to be planned and monitored carefully to ensure that a company has sufficient cash in hand at all times to meet its immediate needs. Failure to meet financial obligations as they come due may be most serious and could lead to bankruptcy.

The running of a business involves the acquisition of assets, purchase of stocks, and payment of wages and other expenses, all of which normally have to be settled by means of cash outgoings. The use of money also incurs outgoings in the form of interest or dividends.

Measures may have to be adopted to enable the company to manage with only small cash balances, thereby releasing the maximum amount of cash for investment in fixed assets and work in progress.

The financial soundness of an organization is of interest not only to the company itself but to many people outside:

1. Creditors will want to know its financial status.
2. Shareholders, banks, and others advancing funds to the company will want to be assured of the security of their investment.
3. A bank loan is much easier to obtain if the bank is satisfied that the cash requirements have been foreseen and estimated in advance.

The planning of cash requirements enables the organization to foresee both surpluses and shortages. If it is anticipated that additional funds will be required at a particular date, it should be possible to choose the most advantageous time to raise share capital or other loans. On the other hand, temporary surplus cash may be used for short-term investments while permanent surplus funds may be used to develop the business by acquiring additional assets, subsidiaries, or ordinary long-term outside investments.

Managing cash flow

B. Check your understanding

Now read the text carefully, looking up in your dictionary anything you do not understand. Then answer the following questions:

1. What is the main cause of failure of businesses?
2. Is the sale of fixed assets a good thing?
3. What is the disadvantage of borrowing money?
4. What is the usual name for forms of cash that can be easily released?
5. What two main factors are involved in effective management of cash?
6. What happens in countries where no debtors are allowed?
7. What is 'age analysis'?
8. What steps can be taken with customers who take too much credit?
9. What does the 80/20 rule state?
10. What may result from failure to meet financial obligations in time?
11. Who is interested in the financial soundness of an organisation?
12. If additional funds are needed, what should be done?
13. What makes a bank more willing to lend money?
14. What use may be made of temporary cash surpluses?
15. How can permanent cash surpluses be used to develop the business?

C. Increase your vocabulary

1. Say in your own words what the following items mean as they are used in the text:

- paragraph 1, line 3: cash resources
             5: creditors

- paragraph 2, lines 5–6: liquidating the capital resources
             line 9: share or stock issues

- paragraph 3, line 10: stock turnover

- paragraph 4, line 12: banker's drafts
             export credit guarantees

- paragraph 5, line 6: acquisition of assets

2. What could you use in this passage instead of the following, without changing the meaning?

- paragraph 1, line 2: generate

- paragraph 2, line 9: mortgages
             overdrafts

- paragraph 4(1), line 1: debtors
             6: stipulation
             12: 'factors'

- paragraph 4(2), line 5: scheduling
             12: capacity
             13: good material flows

10

D. Check your grammar

> **Remember?**
> *This has to be done* at once.
> *You have to do this* at once.

Change the following quotations from the text into the alternative form and explain what difference this makes:

- These have to be paid back.
- The forms of cash that can be released most easily . . .
- An example of the working capital cycle . . . is given.
- It can be seen how rapidly the needs have expanded.
- Standards should be set for typical payment periods.
- Invoices are sent to the customer.
- The planning . . . needs detailed attention.
- It has to be planned and monitored.
- Measures may have to be adopted.
- Temporary surplus cash may be used for short-term investment.

E. Understanding a lecture

You are now going to hear part of a lecture, divided into sections to help you understand it. As you listen to each section, note down what seem to you to be the most important points (there will usually be one major point in each section). The notes do not have to be full sentences: if you try to write complete sentences, the lecturer will have gone on to new points, which you will miss. You can always come back to your notes and expand them after the lecture has finished. Then look at the following questions, which you should also read *before* listening to the lecture, and see if you can answer them, first of all from your notes, and, if not, by replaying the tape. You will find this technique gets easier as you practise it:

1. What does the lecturer say is the aspect that has to be got right — in addition to finance — if a company is to avoid getting into trouble?
2. What government measure controls the registration of companies in the United Kingdom?
3. How many main types of company does the lecturer set out to explain?
4. What is meant by 'unlimited'?
5. In what sort of organisation are you likely to find a company limited by guarantee?
6. What is the aim of such a company?
7. What liability for paying the company's debts does a fully paid up shareholder in a limited company have?
8. What is the minimum value of shares that a company must issue if it wishes to achieve plc status?
9. What do plc and Ltd mean?
10. Is it possible to change from one to another?

F. Understanding a printed text (2)

WORKING CAPITAL

1 Working capital represents funds tied up in the month-by-month operations of the business and as such is the life-line of any firm. An otherwise successful business may be destroyed by a shortage of working capital, which is the most common cause of company failure. Further sales will not be able to save a company that is unable to finance the acquisition or manufacture of the sales themselves.

Working capital = current assets − current liabilities.

Assets

Current assets are represented by

1. Cash.
2. Assets that can be quickly converted into cash, i.e.,
   - Part-finished goods.
   - Finished goods (stocks).
   - Debts, etc.

Liabilities

Current liabilities are those that have to be met in the short term, i.e.,

- Trade creditors.
- Wages and salaries.
- Other expenses.

Budgeting

It is therefore a necessary budgetary exercise to calculate the amount of working capital that will be tied up during the time-cycle of operations, that is, from the time that the first payments have to be made for materials and wages to the time that cash begins to flow in from customers. Factors to be taken into account include such matters as the level of raw materials and finished goods, stock in hand, and the terms of credit taken from and given to suppliers and customers.

Minimizing the amount

2 As capital represents a cost in the form of interest or dividends, efforts should be taken to keep working capital to the minimum consistent with good practice. A number of measures may be adopted to achieve this end, e.g.,

1. A fast production cycle to minimize work in progress.
2. Reduction of stock to optimum levels based on both availability and confidence in the supplier's lead times.
3. Minimum credit given and maximum credit taken.

When a new product is commenced, the working capital requirements increase as the work gets under way and the quantity of work in progress, stock, and debts in the pipeline increases. The peak of working capital requirement may not be reached for several months of operations, and then, if the level of activity starts to level off, so also will the demand for working capital.

3 EXAMPLE OF A WORKING CAPITAL BUDGET

Data

Monthly sales	10 000	
Credit given	2 months	
Monthly purchase of materials	4 000	
Credit obtained thereon	1.5 months	
Stock of materials	1 month	
Finished goods—production cost	8 000 per month	
Stock of finished goods	1 month's supply	
Overheads (1.25 months' credit given)	2 000 per month	

Calculation

Debtors		10 000 × 2	20 000
Stocks: Raw materials		4 000 × 1	4 000
Finished goods		8 000 × 1	8 000
			32 000
Less: Credit received from suppliers of raw materials			
		4 000 × 1	4 000
Other creditors		2 000 × 1.25	2 500
			6 500
Estimated working capital required			25 500

G. Check your understanding

1. Read the text carefully and answer the following questions:
- What is meant by current liabilities?
- If you subtract current liabilities from current assets, what is left?
- Why should working capital be kept to a minimum?
- What happens if business activity levels off?

2. Say whether the following statements are true or not:
- Adequate supply of working capital is vitally important. ☐
- A company which cannot finance its current sales can save itself by increasing them. ☐
- Working capital requirements increase as work on a new product develops. ☐
- Increase of stock in hand reduces the need for working capital. ☐

3. Explain in your own words the meaning of the following:
- paragraph 1, line 2: life-line
- 19: time-cycle
- paragraph 2, line 5: production cycle
- 6: optimum levels
- 7: lead times
- 11: pipeline peak of . . .
- 12: requirement

H. Understanding discourse

Listen to your tape — it may be necessary to play it through several times — on which you will hear two managers talking about their work. (You may find it useful to refer back to section H in Unit 1 before you start.) As you listen, make a note of which managers they are, and of the main divisions they list in each of their departments. Then enter them all on the schemes below and add them to your full scheme in Unit 1.

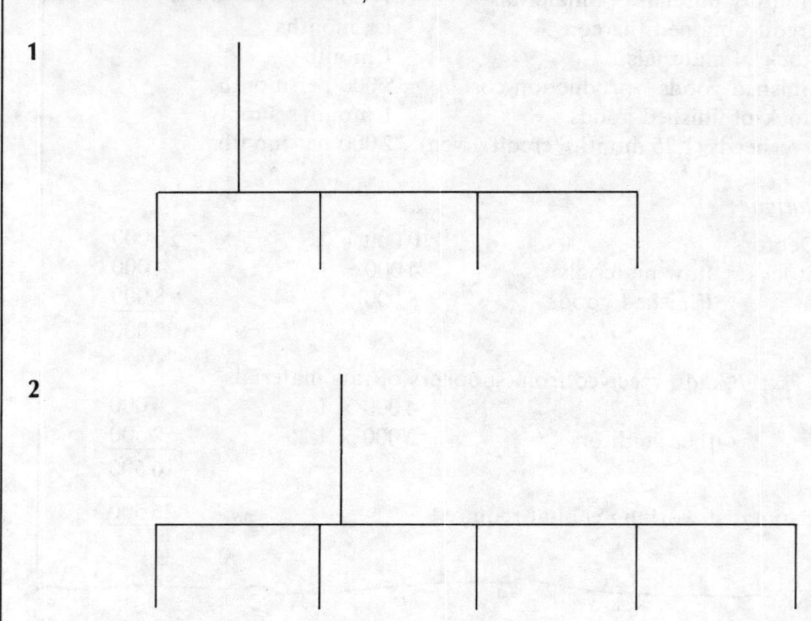

1

2

The passages in parts A and F of this unit are taken from PRABHU and BAKER, *Improving Business Performance*, McGraw Hill, 1986 (edited)

THE PROBLEM OF CASH FLOW (2)

UNIT 3

A. Understanding a printed text (1)

The following passage continues the topic of **the management of cash resources** — the problem of cash flow. Look at the way it is divided into paragraphs, and pay attention to the headings and notes in the margin and to the table.

Now look at the following questions and read through the text quickly to find the answers. Remember, you do not have to understand every word in the text in order to answer the questions:

1. What is the passage about?
2. What two main kinds of credit does it discuss?
3. Which credit cards does it mention?
4. Are credit terms always the same?
5. What is Table 11.2 about?

Trade credit

1 The granting and taking of trade credit is an important and common aspect of business finance.

   Short-term credit helps to smooth business transactions in three ways:

Short-term

   1. Delivery can be made as soon as goods are ready instead of having to store them while arrangements are made for payment.
   2. It is important to settle complaints, make exchanges, and accept returns before payment is due.
   3. Credit transactions require fuller documentation than is needed for cost transactions, so that more complete records have to be kept and internal checks are thereby facilitated.

   Long-term trade credit may be offered to assist customers with limited financial resources. There can be no strong objection to this practice provided that adequate investigation is made into the customers' credit rating. Many businesses, however, are forced by competitive pressures to grant longer periods of credit than they would wish. In cases where the market is highly competitive, quality, price, and delivery may be very finely balanced so that longer credit is the only competitive advantage remaining to the supplier.

Long-term

Methods of payment for goods

2 1. *Cash with order (CWO)*. Cash is paid to the supplier at the time that the order is placed.
2. *Cash on delivery (COD)*. Cash is paid to the supplier at the time of delivery.
3. *Credit account*. The goods are charged to the customer's account on dispatch or after delivery has been accomplished. A limited period of credit is allowed the customer, after the expiry of which he may be charged interest at a specified rate. Discounts may be offered for quick settlement of accounts.
4. *Credit cards*. The credit application is made to the institution that approves the credit and issues the credit card. The business pays a fee to become part of the system. When the sale is made, a credit sales slip is prepared and the business turns this slip over to the institution for cash, receiving the amount of the sale, less a pre-determined charge. Familiar examples of this system are American Express, Access, and Barclaycard Visa.
5. *Extended credit and hire-purchase*. The sale of durable, more expensive, household goods is likely to be restricted unless a company can offer its customers extended terms of some kind. There are a number of possibilities, such as hire-purchase contracts or instalment sales. The legal implication of each case must be considered, as must the current government regulations regarding the initial deposit and the period over which the instalments may be spread.

Normally, the total price paid by the customer is greater when payments are spread over a period than when one immediate cash payment is made. Where payments extend beyond the current financial year, there are two basic methods for allocating the profit earned:

(a) Deemed to be made at time of sale.
(b) Deemed to be made over the life of the contract.

Trade debtors as a source of cash

3 A business having trade debts that will fall due at some future time can often arrange with a financial institution to use these debts as a source of cash. This can be done in three ways:

1. *Pledging the debts*. The financial institution selects certain debts as a pledge against a loan of money to the business. Usually the business collects the accounts and applies the money collected against the loan balance.
2. *Assigning the debts*. The financial institution selects the debts to be used as security for the loan of money to the business. The business may continue to collect the debts and apply the money received against the loan balance, or the lending institution itself may do the collecting. In the latter case this is known as 'factoring' and the institution is known as the 'factor'.
3. *Selling the debts*. In this case the financial institution selects debts and pays the business for those selected. A fee is charged for this service.

4 Credit terms given and offered can vary widely between different customers and suppliers, though in some trades standard terms apply. One of the easiest ways of increasing sales is to increase credit, but it must be appreciated that extending the period of credit increases the amount of working capital required.

Some companies offer discounts to encourage prompt payment, others charge interest on all overdue accounts. In determining its credit policy each company should examine carefully its implications, from the point of view of the company's internal financial position and of its implications in the market-place. Once determined, this policy should be clearly stated at the time of sale.

Typical examples of payment (and therefore credit) terms are:

– Net 30 days after invoice date.
– 2.5 per cent discount if paid before the fifteenth of the month.
– 3.75 per cent discount for payment within seven days of invoice date (standard terms in the shoe and leather industry).
– Payment due by end of month following delivery; thereafter, interest charged at the rate of 2 per cent per month.

Credit policy

5 The maximum utilization of cash resources may be achieved in a number of ways. For example:

1. The use of only one bank balance avoids the dispersal of balances over a number of separate banks.
2. The centralization of accounting functions such as the dispatch of invoices facilitates the accounting work and thereby speeds up the receipt of cash.
3. Customers can be encouraged to pay on receipt of invoice rather than wait for a monthly statement.
4. Accuracy in invoicing should be aimed for, so that customers do not defer payment until a corrected invoice has been received.
5. With a pre-billing rather than a post-billing system, invoices can be sent together with the goods, and credit notes enclosed for any goods that cannot be supplied.
6. Cash discounts can be used to secure early repayments.

Other methods of cash conservation involve:

1. More rapid turnover of stock.
2. Taking maximum credit from suppliers.
3. Disposal of redundant assets at the earliest opportunity.
4. Resorting to hire-purchase arrangements in lieu of outright purchase.
5. Employment of sale-and-lease-back.

Economy of cash resources

Calculation of the cash flow

6 Although the monthly profit and loss forecast will provide some indication of the future direction of the cash flow, it will not show whether sufficient cash will be available to meet commitments as they fall due in the short term. The only satisfactory method of doing this is to provide a cash flow forecast, in which the cash position is determined at the end of each month. In cases where a company is working right up against its credit limits, it may be necessary to calculate the cash position on a weekly basis—say, two weeks in advance.

The following simple example illustrates the presentation of a cash forecast statement.

Data period: 6 months, January–June 198–
Overdraft at 1 January: £50 000

Table 11.2 Cash forecast, six months, January–June 198–

	Jan.	Feb.	Mar.	Apr.	May	June
				£'000		
Payments						
Raw materials supplies	80	80	90	90	70	80
Wages	40	40	40	40	42	40
Sundry creditors	10	10	10	10	10	10
Dividends	50	—	—	—	—	—
Taxes	60	—	—	—	—	—
Capital expenditure	—	40	—	20	40	—
Total cash disbursements	240	170	140	160	162	130
Receipts from debtors	160	160	160	200	200	160
Sale of asset	50	—	—	—	—	—
Cash (surplus) deficit for period	30	10	(20)	(40)	(38)	(30)
Overdraft brought forward	50	80	90	70	50	(8)
Total overdraft requirement at end of month	80	90	70	30	(8)	(38)

A capital expenditure project has been sanctioned to the value of £100 000 which will involve instalments of £40 000 and £20 000 in February and April, respectively, with the balance payable in May. Receipts from debtors are expected to amount to £16 000 per month, increasing to £20 000 in April and May. The sale of a piece of land is expected to fetch £50 000 in January. Settlements with creditors (for expenses, etc.) will run at £10 000 per month. Wages amount to £40 000 per month with an anticipated addition of £2000 in May. Payments to suppliers of raw materials amount to £80 000 per month, rising to £90 000 in March and April and falling to £70 000 in May. Table 11.2 shows how to calculate the amount of overdraft that will be required each month to meet the companies' needs.

B. Check your understanding

Read through the passage carefully, looking up anything you do not understand. Then answer the following questions:

1. What effect does short-term credit have on the delivery of goods?
2. Why do credit sales require more documentation than cash sales?
3. Is there any objection to granting long-term credit to customers with limited cash resources?
4. When may firms be forced to give longer-term credit than they would wish?
5. What do the abbreviation CWO and COD mean? Explain the difference.
6. What credit cards do you know of?
7. What may restrict the sale of expensive household goods?
8. What is the normal effect for the borrower of spreading payment over a period of time?
9. What is meant by 'factoring'?
10. What is the effect on working capital if credit terms are extended?
11. What is a typical term of credit?
12. What discount is offered in the leather trade on payments made within 7 days of invoice?
13. What would be the effect on cash resources of selling stock more quickly?
14. What is the only satisfactory way to show that sufficient cash will be available to meet financial commitments?
15. In the cash forecast in Table 11.2, what is the most costly single item?

C. Increase your vocabulary

Check in your dictionary, then say in your own words what the following mean as used in the text:

- paragraph 1, line 3: transactions
  - 13: credit rating
  - 16: finely balanced
- paragraph 2, line 8: at a specified rate
  - 12: credit sales slip
  - 14: pre-determined charge
  - 17: durable (goods)
  - 18: extended terms
  - 20: hire-purchase contracts
    instalment sales
  - 27: allocating
  - 28: deemed
- paragraph 3, line 4: pledging
  - 8: assigning
- paragraph 4, line 7: credit policy
- paragraph 5, line 12: pre-billing
  - 20: in lieu of
  - 21: sale-and-lease-back
- Table 11.2, line 4: sundry
  - line 8: disbursements

D. Check your grammar

> **Remember?**
> *Delivery can be made at once.*
> *You can make delivery/deliver at once.*

Give the alternative versions for the following quotations from the text:
- arrangements are made for payment . . .
- complaints must be settled . . .
- sufficient cash must be on hand . . .
- the cash position may have to be calculated . . .
- long-term credit may be offered . . .
- there can be no objection . . .
- provided that adequate investigation is made . . .
- the goods are charged to the customer's account . . .
- each case must be considered . . .

E. Understanding a lecture

Listen to the lecture on your tape. It has been divided into sections to make it easier for you to understand. Look at the questions below, then play through the tape and make notes for the answers. You can then expand your notes into full sentences:

Section 1
- What does the lecturer say he is going to explain today?
- What name is given to the people who are going to start a new company?
- What has to be done with the documents when they are completed?

Section 2
- What does the Memorandum of Association define?
- In what circumstances can the Registrar of Companies refuse to accept a proposed title?
- What is the official name of a company's legal home?
- Does the company have to carry on its business there?

Section 3
- What part of the document says what the purpose of the company is?

Section 4
- What is nominal capital?

Section 5
- How many shares must a shareholder own?

Section 6
- What document lays down the internal procedures of a company?
- If a company does not submit this document, what is it presumed to have adopted?

F. Understanding a printed text (2)

CREDIT CONTROL

1 The credit control function should be the responsibility of a credit manager backed up by a dedicated team. The credit manager plays a vital role within the company, for it is his responsibility to see that customers pay for their goods and services within the agreed time and that they are not allowed to take unauthorized credit. His prime role may therefore be described as maintaining the momentum of cash flow into the company.

Systematic credit control

The credit manager is likely to be pulled in two opposing directions: by the sales managers, seeking to increase the amount of credit given in order to gain sales, and by the accountant, wishing to ensure that the company is paid for every sale made.

The main tasks of a credit manager are:

1. Setting customer credit levels.
2. Releasing customers' orders.
3. Analysing accounts outstanding for extended credit-taking.
4. Chasing overdue accounts for payment.
5. Conducting an age analysis of outstanding accounts.
6. Monitoring total credit outstanding.

2 The credit level granted to a customer will depend on that customer's financial standing. Granting credit always implies some degree of risk as the customer could default in payment. In most cases this risk is very small if the company deals only with customers of known repute. Credit ratings of new customers can be determined from banks or credit-rating bureaux.

Setting customer credit level

It must be appreciated, however, that the more credit is granted, the greater is the working capital required.

3 When an order is received by a company, after it has been checked by the sales department, it is passed to credit control before being released into the order system.

Releasing customers' orders

In credit control a payment history is kept of each customer together with his credit limit, and if the *new order does not take him above this limit* the order is released. If not, then the customer is contacted and the order held until payment has been made to open up the account sufficiently for the order to be accepted.

In practice, the credit manager will often exercise his discretion with well-known customers and authorize (temporarily) a higher credit limit in order to clear the order. It is usually in the company's interest to expedite the order as quickly as possible, provided that the credit manager is confident of being paid in full for it.

4 The credit manager either will have access to the customers' accounts on the sales ledger through the data processing system, or will maintain his own records on hard copy of customers' invoices that have become overdue for payment, and will set in motion the follow-up system. Different types of customer may be given varying credit terms, and each account should be signalled as soon as its credit period has expired.

Analysing account outstanding for extended credit-taking

▼

Chasing overdue accounts for payment

5 A reminder should be sent to the customer as soon as he fails to pay by the due date. Reminders should be made frequently, say, every seven days, and should be made more forceful as time goes by. The ultimate step is to threaten to take court action and put the matter into the hands of a solicitor. Alternatively, the debt can be put into the hands of a debt collection agency, which will charge a fee for its services.

In many cases of non-payment the matter can be satisfactorily settled before the full course has been run by personal contact with the recalcitrant customer, and it pays to establish a friendly relationship with the individual who is responsible for authorizing payment of the outstanding account. Do not, however, fall for the perennial ploy, 'I have put a cheque in the post this morning.'

Conducting age-analysis of oustanding accounts

6 An analysis should be regularly undertaken of the age of all outstanding invoices. A table can be drawn up showing the amounts outstanding by a customer by week of invoice date, and the totals for each week can be plotted to give a credit profile showing the relationship between the total money outstanding and the length of credit (in weeks) taken. A typical format for an age analysis is shown in Fig. 11.2.

Alternatively, the data processing system may be able to throw up totals for each week-band so that the age profile can be drawn together with details of all invoices that are overdue for payment.

Monitoring total credit outstanding

7 The total credit outstanding will be related to the volume of recent sales, and as sales rise the volume of credit is likely to rise in a similar fashion. The most suitable measure of success of the credit control operation, therefore, is to express the credit outstanding in terms of the number of days' sales that it represents.

If the standard credit terms are 20 working days, then the target to aim for is that the total cash outstanding should be equal to the last 20 days' sales. Almost inevitably, the actual figure will be more than 20 days as customers will take more credit than they are entitled to, but every effort must be made to bring the figure in to as close to 20 as possible.

Customer	Inv. no.	1	2	3	4	5	6	7	8	9	10	11	12	13	14	15	16	17	18	19	20	Remarks
Alpha Co.	246		100																			
	202						200															
	176												100									
Beta Co.	241		50																			
	203						150															
	189									200												
Gamma Co.	20																				200	Account stopped
Delta Co.	210					200																
	152													100								
Epsilon Co.	271	150																				
	204			100																		
	225					150																
Totals																						

Fig. 11.2 Typical format for an age analysis profile

G. Check your understanding

1. Read the text carefully and answer the following questions:
- What is the prime role of the credit manager?
- Do credit managers and sales managers always agree?
- Who is responsible for chasing overdue accounts for payment?
- How does granting credit involve risk?
- Who keeps the record of a customer's payment history?
- When might a credit manager authorise a higher credit limit?
- Do all customers get the same terms?
- What is the ultimate step if a customer does not pay?
- What is 'age-analysis'?
- Do customers ever take longer to pay than they are entitled to?

2. Say whether the following statements are true or not true:

The credit manager is not concerned with cash flow.	☐
There is no risk in granting credit to new customers.	☐
It is usually in the company's interest to service orders as quickly as possible.	☐
The volume of credit rises with the volume of sales.	☐

H. Understanding discourse

Listen to your tape, on which you will hear two more managers discussing their work. Note down the titles of the managers and the names of the chief divisions they mention within their departments. Add these to the schemes below and then add them to the composite scheme in Unit 1.

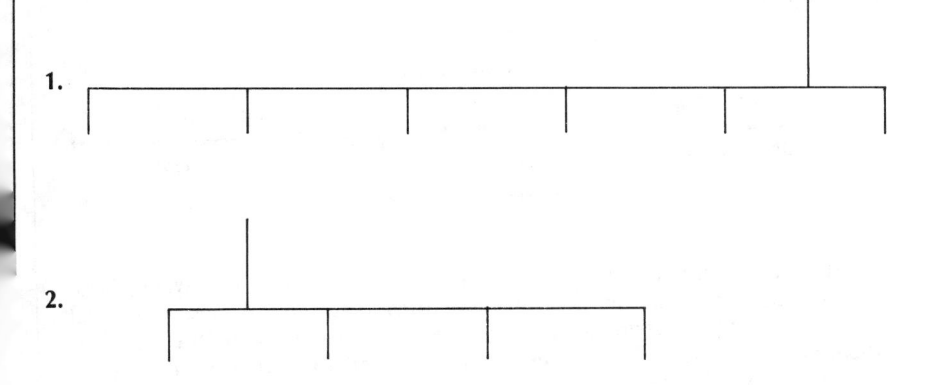

1.

2.

3 Now answer the following questions.
- What does the first speaker mean by 'skinflint'?
- What does he mean when he says that he has to 'axe . . . pet schemes'?
- What is the biggest single recurring item of expense?
- What does 'slimming down' mean?
- Why does the second speaker think that buying too much raw material is bad for business?
- What do you understand by 'time . . . means money'?

The passages in parts A and F of this unit are taken (edited) from PRABHU and BAKER, *Improving Business Performance*, McGraw Hill, 1986

UNIT 4

THE PAPER CHASE

A. Understanding a printed text (1)

The following text introduces the topic of the different functional areas within a business and the importance of keeping the necessary paper work — **information flow** — moving efficiently. Look at the construction of the passage and pay attention to the marginal headings and the illustrations and captions.

Then look at the following questions and read through the text quickly in order to find the answers. Remember, you do not have to understand every word in the passage in order to answer the questions:

1 What is the passage about?
2 What is a functional business area?
3 What four areas are dealt with in the passage?
4 Why is it important to keep information flowing between the areas?

Business functional areas

Information and the business

HOW A BUSINESS IS ORGANISED

1 Whatever the nature of a small business, there are many functions that are common between it and business in general. All businesses provide either products or services that have to be sold on the market in order that the business can survive. To produce goods or services, a business needs to buy goods or services. A business, therefore, has to interact with many agencies in the outside world and information has to flow between the business and these outside agencies (Fig. 1.1).

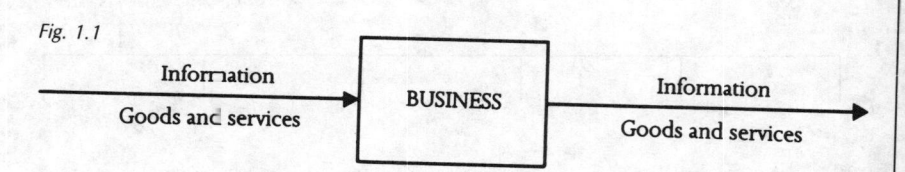

Fig. 1.1

Information → BUSINESS → Information
Goods and services → → Goods and services

Within the business there are also many information flows between those areas concerned with the different functions that the business's internal organization has to perform, i.e., information flows between the different functional areas within the business. A functional area is that group of internal business activities concerned with a particular business function; for example, the sales or accounts function. To illustrate and explain this some typical functional areas will be considered and the information flows concerned with these areas will be described.

24

2 All businesses will be concerned to sell their services or products. In order to do this a business will need to interact with its customers. The customers will place orders and the sales area will process the order so that the customer is satisfied. When this has happened, sales will notify the accounts functional area which will initiate the accounts procedures (Fig. 1.2).

Sales

```
Fig. 1.2        Customer order
                ───────────────►
   CUSTOMER                         SALES      Copy of customer order    ACCOUNTS
                ◄───────────────                ──────────────────────►
                  Confirmation
              (copy of customer order)
```

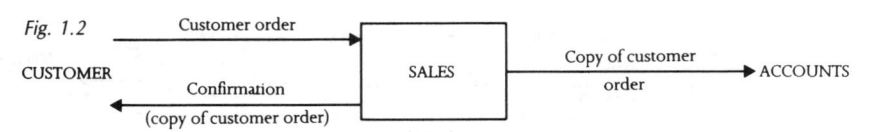

Information flows into and out of the sales functional area

From Fig. 1.2 it can be seen that the customer initiates an order by sending an order form to the sales area (in a real-life situation the customer might make an order with a salesman or might send the order by telephone). The sales area responds with a notification that the order has been received and later sends a copy of the order to the accounts area for customer invoice and billing. The arrowed lines in the diagram represent the information flows into and out of the sales functional area.

3 This is concerned with the materials inputs to the business. It is responsible for purchasing all the raw materials and finished products from suppliers in order that the business can perform its production or service function. This area places purchase orders with suppliers and notifies accounts which will settle the bill when the order has been satisfied and the bill has been received.

Purchasing

```
Fig. 1.3         Purchase order
                ◄───────────────
   SUPPLIER                        PURCHASING    Copy of purchase order    ACCOUNTS
                ───────────────►                ──────────────────────►
                  Confirmation
```

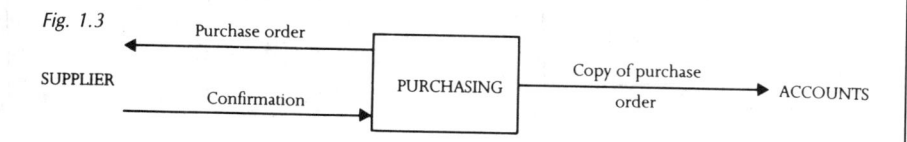

Information flows into and out of the purchasing functional area

Again, the purchase order details and the confirmation details represent the information flows between the purchasing functional area and the supplier and the purchasing functional area and accounts.

Accounts

4 This is responsible for handling the financial side of the business operations. It will issue invoices and bills to customers, receive invoices and bills from suppliers and receive information from and issue information to other internal functional areas which help it perform its function, receive payments from customers, issue credit notes to customers, receive credit notes from suppliers and make payments to suppliers (Fig. 1.4).

Information flows into and out of the accounts functional area

Fig. 1.4

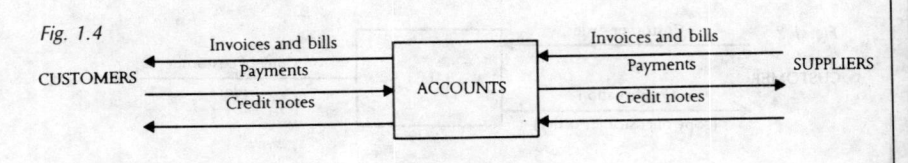

CUSTOMERS — Invoices and bills / Payments / Credit notes — ACCOUNTS — Invoices and bills / Payments / Credit notes — SUPPLIERS

5 The relationship between sales, purchasing and accounts can be represented as shown in Fig. 1.5.

Information diagram for the sales, purchasing and accounts functional areas

Fig. 1.5

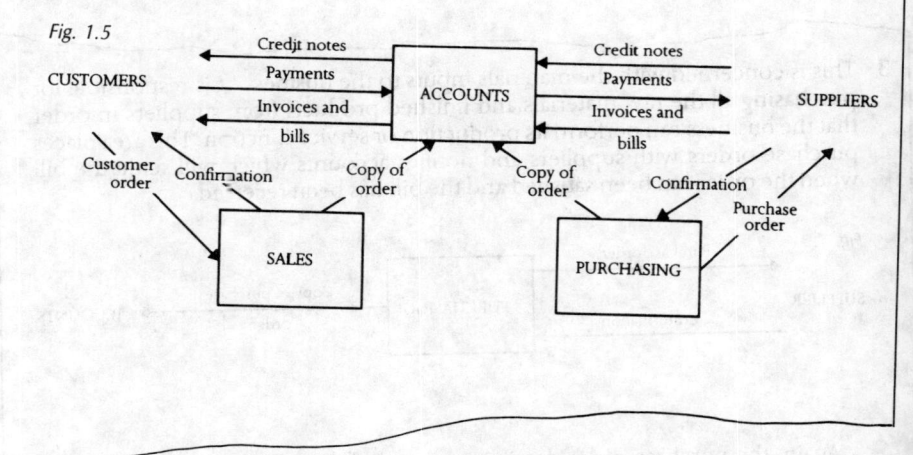

CUSTOMERS — Credit notes / Payments / Invoices and bills — ACCOUNTS — Credit notes / Payments / Invoices and bills — SUPPLIERS

Customer order / Confirmation — SALES — Copy of order

Copy of order — PURCHASING — Confirmation / Purchase order

6 This area is concerned with maintaining a current up-to-date list or inventory of stock held by a business. The stock inventory allows a manufacturing business, for instance, to maintain sufficient stock to satisfy the production area so that it can complete its work efficiently and satisfy its customers' orders. It also allows a supplier of finished products to provide its customers with an efficient service.

For example, a wholesale organization needs to keep sufficient stock in all categories to be able to supply its customers, the retailers, without unnecessary delays. But stock held by a wholesaler costs a great deal of money. Over-stocking has to be avoided; it ties up capital and affects cash flow. Therefore, it is necessary to estimate as accurately as possible the levels of stock for each item held to balance the opposing pressures of minimizing necessary stock on the one hand and holding enough stock to reduce delays for the customers on the other.

When stock levels fall re-orders have to be initiated via the purchasing functional area. The level for each item of stock has to be updated when deliveries of new stock arrive via the goods inward functional area and when stock is sent to the transport or shipping functional area for delivery to customers or when stock is used by production or other functional areas. The maintenance of a stock inventory allows stock enquiries to be made and at certain periods it allows stock valuations and checks to be carried out.

Stock control

The relationship between the stock-control and other functional areas is shown in Fig. 1.6.

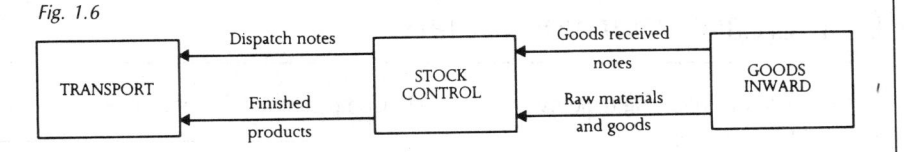

Fig. 1.6

TRANSPORT ←Dispatch notes— STOCK CONTROL ←Goods received notes— GOODS INWARD
            —Finished products→   ←Raw materials and goods—

Information diagram for the stock control functional area

The stock control function is often separated from the warehouse or stores function. The former is concerned with maintaining an inventory of stock currently held while the latter is concerned wth the physical storage of the goods.

B. Check your understanding

1. Now read the passage carefully, looking up anything you do not understand. Then answer the following questions:

1. What functions do all businesses have in common?
2. What must a business do in order to sell its product or services?
3. Which business area processes orders?
4. Which area starts accounts procedures?

5. Name two of the ways in which a customer may place an order.
6. Why does the sales area send a copy of the customer's order to the accounts area?
7. From Figure 1.2, what does the customer first receive after placing an order?
8. What is the concern of the purchase area?
9. How does it ensure that the business can perform its production function?
10. What does the accounts area issue to customers?
11. What is the purpose of a stock inventory?
12. What effect does it have on the supplier of finished products?
13. Why should over-stocking be avoided?
14. What must be done when new stocks arrive?
15. What is the function of a warehouse?

2. Look at Figures 1.1–1.6 and say:
- What is the flow of information between business and goods and services?
- What does the customer receive after placing an order?
- To whom are copies of purchase orders supplied?
- What is the distribution of credit notes?
- What is the route of a customer order?
- Trace the progress of raw materials in a business.

C. Increase your vocabulary

1. Complete the following table by supplying the missing words:

Verb	Noun
notify	notification
	interaction
	information
explain	
illustrate	
consider	
describe	
satisfy	
initiate	
	confirmation
	organisation
	situation
represent	
	production
	operation
estimate	
oppose	
provide	

2. Complete the following table:

e.g. *necessary*	*unnecessary*
	uncommon
satisfied	
typical	
finished	
sufficient	
accurately	
possible	

NB: If several words are possible, give them all and explain the difference in meaning, if any.

D. Check your grammar

In the following references to the passage, say what the words indicated refer to:

- paragraph 1, line 2: it
             13: this
             15: these areas

- paragraph 3, line 1: it
             3: its

- paragraph 4, line 4: it

- paragraph 6, line 3: it
             4: its, it
             5: its
             7: its
             9: it
             18: it

E. Understanding a lecture

Listen to the lecture on your tape. It is divided into a number of short sections to make it easier to understand. Then look at the questions below and listen to the tape again, section by section, making notes of the answers. You can fill out your notes into complete statements afterwards, to form a short summary of the lecture.

Section 1
- What is to be the topic of the lecture?

Section 2
- What is meant by 'share capital'?
- What has to be stated in the Memorandum of Association?

Section 3
- What does 'nominal capital' mean?
- How is it different from 'issued capital'?

Section 4
- In what circumstances may your shares be worth more than you paid for them?
- Can they also sometimes be worth less?

Section 5
- Why should a company keep at least as much capital as it raised by sale of shares?

Section 6
- How does a company invite people to buy shares?

Section 7
- Does a shareholder have to consult the company if he wants to sell his shares in it?
- What regulates the procedures for the sale of shares?

Section 8
- What is the point of buying shares?
- From what sources must dividends be paid?

F. Understanding a printed text (2)

MORE FUNCTIONAL AREAS

Goods inward

1 This is responsible for the receipt of goods and raw materials with accompanying documentation. When items are received the stock control functional area is informed using a goods received note indicating that they are now available for satisfaction of customer orders or for entry into the production process (Fig. 1.7).

Information diagram for the goods inward functional area

Fig. 1.7

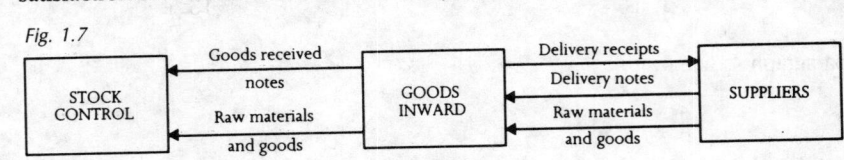

STOCK CONTROL ← Goods received notes / Raw materials and goods ← GOODS INWARD ← Delivery receipts / Delivery notes / Raw materials and goods ← SUPPLIERS

The information flow is represented by the delivery note and goods received note documents.

Transport and shipping

2 On the receipt of a dispatch note from the sales functional area, the transport and shipping functional area will package and send by road, rail, sea, air or any combination of these, the goods that the customer orders with all necessary documentation (Fig. 1.8).

Information diagram for the transport and shipping functional area

Fig. 1.8

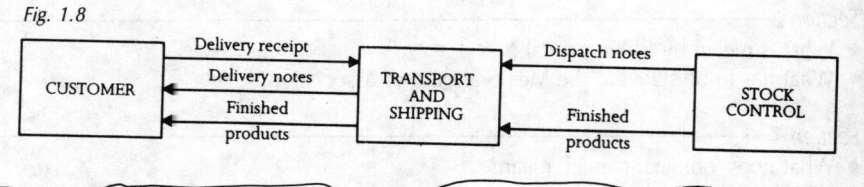

CUSTOMER ← Delivery receipt / Delivery notes / Finished products ← TRANSPORT AND SHIPPING ← Dispatch notes / Finished products ← STOCK CONTROL

Production

3 This is responsible for the production of goods. It will receive orders from the sales functional area and materials from stock, return finished goods to stock for shipping to customers and issue purchase requisitions to purchasing with a copy to the stock control functional area. It may also receive production designs via the engineering functional area from research and development (Fig. 1.9).

Information diagram for the production functional area

Fig. 1.9

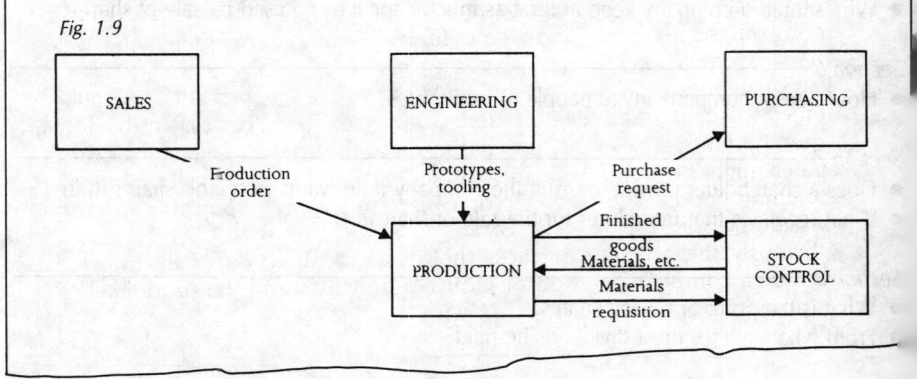

SALES → Production order → PRODUCTION
ENGINEERING → Prototypes, tooling → PRODUCTION
PRODUCTION → Purchase request → PURCHASING
PRODUCTION → Finished goods Materials, etc. → STOCK CONTROL
STOCK CONTROL → Materials requisition → PRODUCTION

4   Figure 1.9 could be further expanded to include the costing or financial estimating functional area. All new designs from the engineering functional area would be costed and details sent to accounts (see Fig. 1.10).

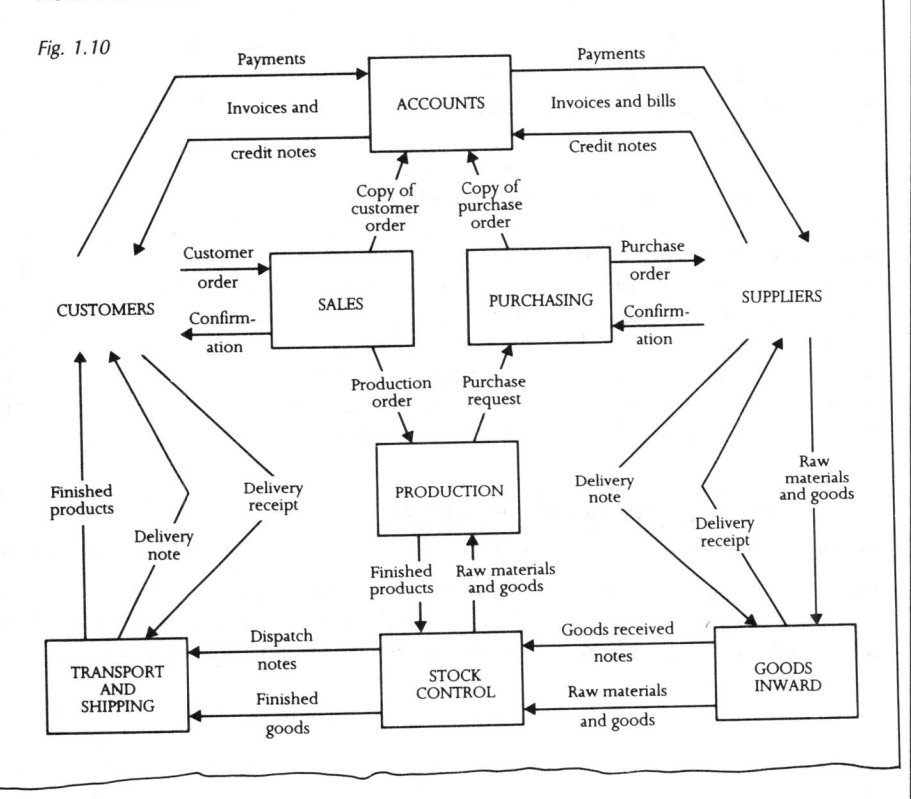

Fig. 1.10

Information diagram showing relationships between the production, transport and shipping, stock control, goods inward, sales, purchasing and accounts functional area

5 Business departments

It is important that the concept of business functional areas does not get confused with the idea of a business department. In a large organization, each business function is likely to be more efficiently carried out by a separate department. There will for instance be an accounts department, a sales department, a purchasing or buying department, a dispatch department, probably also combining the goods inward function, as well as departments for carrying out the personnel and salaries functions. Each department will have its own management structure.

In a small business, however, the functions will be grouped and it is unlikely that they will be departmentally based. One person might be responsible for all accounting functions – sales, purchasing, accounting – as well as for salaries. Another might be responsible for handling physical stock – for receiving and dispatching goods. The manager or owner might be responsible for some production work.

Obviously, the larger the business, the greater the difficulty for any individual to handle a complete function or group of functions and the more likely for departments to appear.

G. Check your understanding

1. Read the text carefully and answer the following questions:
- What document does the stock control area receive to show that goods or materials are available?
- What must the transport area receive before it will send goods to the customer?
- What else does it send to the customer?
- Who orders goods from the production area?
- What happens to new designs?

2. Say whether the following statements are true or not:
- Delivery notes are sent from the supplier to stock control. ☐
- The transport area will not send goods without a dispatch note. ☐
- Dispatch notes are sent from the accounts area to transport and shipping. ☐
- Purchase requests are sent by the purchasing area to stock control. ☐
- The accounts area is notified of the cost of new designs. ☐
- Business functional areas and business departments are the same. ☐
- Departments usually have their own management structures. ☐
- The larger the business, the more likely it is to be split into departments. ☐

H. Understanding discourse

Listen to your tape, on which you will hear the last two managers discussing their work. Note down what their departments are and what main divisions they mention within them. Then add these to the schemes below and complete the composite scheme in Unit 1.

1

2

The passages in sections A and F of this unit were taken (edited) from HUDSON and BATTEN, *Business Systems*, McGraw Hill, 1982

LIES AND STATISTICS

UNIT 5

A. Understanding a printed text (1)

The following text introduces the topic of **statistics for marketing**. Look at the way it is organised and pay attention to the headings, illustrations and captions. Then look at these questions and read the passage through. Remember, you do not have to understand every word in order to answer the questions:

1. Why are the statistics sometimes compared with lies?
2. What are the chief dangers referred to in the title?
3. What quality should a manager have in order to be able to use statistics correctly?

HIDDEN DANGERS

1. The most frequently quoted remark about statistics is probably: 'There are lies, damned lies and statistics.' The dangers of interpreting percentages is beautifully illustrated by the invention of an imaginary advertisement for a 'Rabbitburger'. Everyone knows what a Hamburger is. The Rabbitburger, it was claimed, was 50% rabbit and 50% horse, which investigation revealed as meaning that it was made from a ratio of meat of one rabbit to one horse!

2. The manager does not have to be a professional statistician, nor does he have to be frightened by the statisticians any more than by economists or the biochemists. However, he cannot afford to be a literate linguist; he must be adequately numerate. Statistics are not only used by Marketing people. The principles apply universally.

3. In forecasting, one's *prognosis* may derive from extrapolation of previous trends. The very numerate may be quite happy to see the figures in a *table* or in some tabular form. Ordinary *mortals* find it helpful to see the trends portrayed on a graph. This can be dangerous, particularly if a graph is shown of only a part of the curve. One frequently sees a chart like this:

```
2.1856
2.1855
2.1854
2.1853
```

One's first reaction might be: 'Good heavens, what fluctuations!' Then one looks again and realises that we are only looking at the very top of the whole graph and if we used the whole of this page on the same scale we would only be plotting a range between about 2.1847 and 2.1867, a difference of 0.0020, or a fifth of 1%. Our chart shows a fraction of that. So one has to be very careful not to be misled by graphs.

The Rabbitburger

Literacy and numeracy

The dangers of graphs

Setting the parameters

4   The first thing to get clear, then, in a graph is the scale to be used for the parameters. The horizontal scale will often represent time, while the vertical will register totals. In Supply and Demand curves the vertical generally registers price and the horizontal figure represents Supply or Demand in units of one kind or another, tons, tonnes, volume, etc. So the two arms of a right angle represent the parameters for our diagrammatic presentation of information.

One way of showing percentages of a whole is by using a pie chart, which is merely the circumference of a circle with segments representing the various percentages.

Pie charts

5   The pie chart is an excellent example of how business people, with limited experience, can scare themselves by not knowing the jargon. One manager, asked to present his information on a pie chart, got into a panic thinking that he would have to do lots of complicated calculations with $2\pi r$ and πr^2. Eventually he plucked up courage to ask what a pie chart was and what it looked like and was relieved to learn that is was called a pie chart because it was the shape of a custard pie! Proportions of revenue or expenditure are often shown in this way in company reports — say 45% for labour, 30% for materials, and 25% for depreciation of capital assets. We do not have to be very clever to appreciate that a segment with an obtuse angle at the apex would represent more than 25% and one with an acute angle would represent less than 25%.

Sectors and segments

6   Since we may come across the terms 'sector' and 'segment' in business terminology, it may be as well to remind ourselves of our elementary geometry and how they are used in chopping up circles:

Figure 1

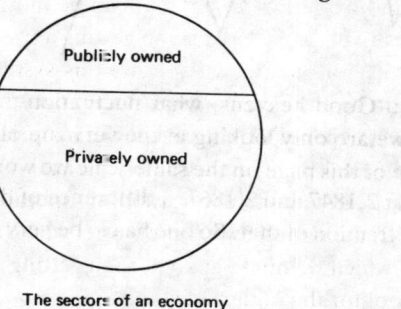

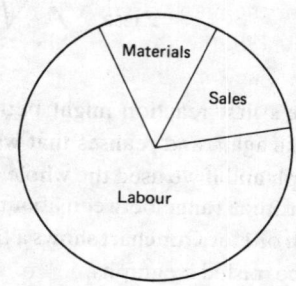

The sectors of an economy (Publicly owned / Privately owned)

The segments of a company's costs (Materials, Sales, Labour)

34

7 Another simple way of showing totals is on a bar chart, the height of each bar representing larger or smaller amounts. A bar chart representing proportions of a total or a series of totals is called a histogram, from which can be determined the shape of a distribution curve.

Bar charts

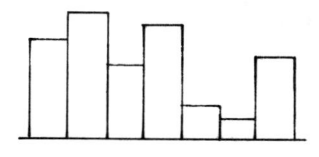

8 Percentages do not present us with much difficulty so long as we remember *what* percentage of *what* we are talking about and remember that you cannot calculate a percentage of percentages and expect to have anything with any meaning. Averages may be more difficult in that we have to know what kind of average our statistician is feeding us with. A 'mean' is an arithmetical average.

The perils of percentages

9 For example, if we have ten guinea-pigs, and we divide the total *weight* of the animals by the total *number* of animals, we should arrive at the mean weight. However, if in our sample group there happened to be a giant-sized guinea-pig, he would distort the average (ie mean), so as to make it a meaningless statistic. Similarly, one underfed guinea-pig in the sample would cause a deviation from the mean, although it would not distort the mean as much as the giant weighing many times more than the average. In order that the average should not be unduly distorted causing a *skew* as against a normal distribution curve, we can ignore the exceptions but then we no longer have a mean average, but a median. In addition, should we for some obscure reason want to fit all our guinea-pigs with woolly jackets and not want to have to buy too many different sizes, we must find out which size occurs most frequently and that size will be neither the mean nor the median; it will be the mode. All, technically, are averages (see Figure 2).

Skewing the curve

10 Silly mistakes can be made by using the wrong average. Going back to those jackets for our guinea-pigs, we can save ourselves money by buying the right size for the maximum number and by getting a size that can be most cheaply modified for the minority. Alternatively, this could mean getting a size to fit the biggest, and modifying the rest. With our outsize fellow, this system would make it very expensive and it might be more economical to buy coats that would be right for the next biggest. Much depends on the cost of the material and the cost of modification, but the statistical techniques of arriving at the optimum size of coat to be bought in bulk is, in fact, an application of Operational Research. Referring back to Figure 2, the right size of jacket to get would probably be the one for the 4-pounder, of which we might get ten, then getting a blanket for the giant and some cotton wool for the underfed guinea-pig.

Choosing the right average

Figure 2
TEN LITTLE GUINEA-PIGS
(and one big one)

Weight of the animals:

No. 1	3.75 lb
No. 2	3.75 lb
No. 3	3.75 lb
No. 4	3.95 lb
No. 5	3.55 lb
No. 6	4.00 lb
No. 7	0.25 lb
No. 8	3.75 lb
No. 9	3.75 lb
No. 10	15.00 lb
No. 11	4.00 lb
Total weight	49.50 lb

Mean weight $= \dfrac{49.5}{11}$ = the average weight of all the animals   4·5 lb

Median weight $= 49.5 - 0.25 - 15.0 = \dfrac{34.25}{9} = 3.806 =$ the average weight of all the animals except the biggest and the smallest   3.81 lb

Mode weight $= 3.75$ lb = the most frequent occurring weight of the animals (5 times)   3.75 lb

GLOSSARY

prognosis — forecast
mortals — people are not immortal; one day they will die.
table — a chart with a list of figures
skew — distortion

B. Check your understanding

1. Now re-read the text carefully, looking up anything you do not understand, and answer the following questions:

1. What would you expect a Rabbitburger to contain?
2. Why was the claim of 50% rabbit and 50% horse misleading?
3. What is the chief danger in interpreting a graph?
4. What is meant by the 'parameters' of a graph?
5. What does the vertical usually represent in a Supply and Demand curve?
6. What is a pie chart?
7. What is the most important question to ask when dealing with percentages?
8. What is a mean weight?
9. What is a median?
10. What is a mode?

2. Say whether the following statements are true or not true:

1. Business managers should all be professional statisticians. ☐
2. Prognosis relies a lot on analysis of trends. ☐
3. Numerate people can interpret tables easily. ☐
4. Graphs can be dangerously misleading to people who cannot interpret them correctly. ☐
5. A pie chart is simply a circle cut into segments representing percentages. ☐
6. Quoting a percentage is meaningless if you do not state what it is a percentage of. ☐
7. Including one very odd example in a group will distort the average. ☐
8. If the exceptions are left out, the result is the mean average. ☐
9. The most common size etc. in a sample is the mode. ☐
10. Technically, means, medians and modes are all averages. ☐

C. Increase your vocabulary

Explain in your own words what the following words or expressions mean as used in the text. You may need to refer to a dictionary.

- paragraph 1, lines 2–3: beautifully illustrated

- paragraph 2, line 3: literate
            4: numerate

- paragraph 3, line 1: extrapolation
            3: tabular
            6: fluctuations

- paragraph 5, line 5: plucked up courage
            10: obtuse angle
            11: acute angle

- paragraph 10, line 8: optimum

D. Check your grammar

> **Remember**
> a. This can be done in several ways.
> b. You can do this in several ways.
> c. One can do this in several ways.

Now fill in the two other versions for each of the following:

1. a. _____
   b. _____
   c. One can frequently see a chart like this.

2. a. _____
   b. _____
   c. One has to take great care not to be misled by graphs.

3. a. _____
   b. You can ignore the exceptions.
   c. _____

4. a. The best size can quite easily be calculated.
   b. _____
   c. _____

5. a. _____
   b. You can save yourself money by buying the right size.
   c. _____

E. Understanding a lecture

Listen to the lecture on your tape. It is divided into sections so that you can listen to them separately. First play the lecture right though, to hear what it is all about; then look at the questions below and play the tape again, one section at a time. Make notes for answers to the questions, then write them up as complete sentences.

Section 1
- What is the point of all the paperwork that circulates inside a company?

Section 2
- What should go into a catalogue?

Section 3
- How does a customer order something?

Section 4
- What does he receive with the goods?
- What does he receive if the goods are 'on approval'?
- What do you think 'on approval' means?

Section 5
- What is the purpose of a statement?
- How often are statements sent out?

Section 6
- How would you find out whether a company can supply what you want?

Section 7
- How would you find out what it would cost you?

F. Understanding a printed text (2)

SAMPLING THE MARKET

1 How is sampling for Market Research carried out? We all know that if we have a thousand beans, beads, or other objects of, say, five different colours in a jar and pick out ten or so at random, provided the beans have been well shaken up, the ten in the selection we make at random from the jar will be roughly in the same proportion to the totals. This is of course how polling is done. A cross-section of the population is asked a question, or a series of questions, and the answers will be *roughly* in proportion to the answers you would get from the whole population. The word population is used in statistics whether we are talking of humans, animals, or coloured beans. The sample will not reflect the position of the whole population absolutely accurately, as we know well from predictions of what will happen at elections. The bigger the sample the more like the total it will be and thus more accurate. Experiments show, however, that the degree of accuracy does not increase appreciably after one has obtained the minimum satisfactory size of sample.

Conducting a poll

The questionnaire

2 Sample consumers can be asked to answer a questionnaire about their reactions. The people who ask the questions for these surveys are generally women. They are usually more gentle and sympathetic, and people are less likely to tell them to *jump in the lake*. They will be asked to put the questions to a representative sample of potential users of the product who will have been selected according to their socio-economic categorisation on a scale from A for the richest to E for the poorest with subdivisions within each group from 1 to 3. If the questionnaire is about expensive cars, for instance, they would approach the A/B socio-economic groups and not C/D/E. They will keep a *tally* of the answers or their observations, or maybe the person analysing the answers would do this simply by marking a diagonal stroke (/) for every occurrence of each category of answer or observation. The tally would look like this: ////. After the fifth reply, the marker would put a line through the tally thus: ////, and start again. The tally would then be put in the form of a histogram thus:

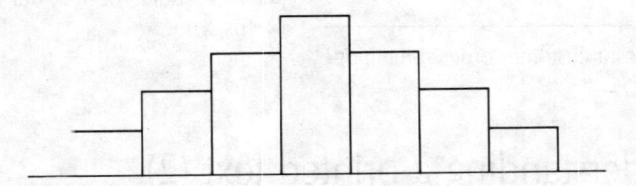

Distribution curve

3 That is the sort of pattern you would get if you were measuring the heights of 15-year-old boys. Plotted onto a graph this describes a normal distribution curve, as we can see just by joining the tops of the bars. In fact, statisticians do not make their curves quite like that. They plot the curve by cutting the same area from each side of the histogram so:

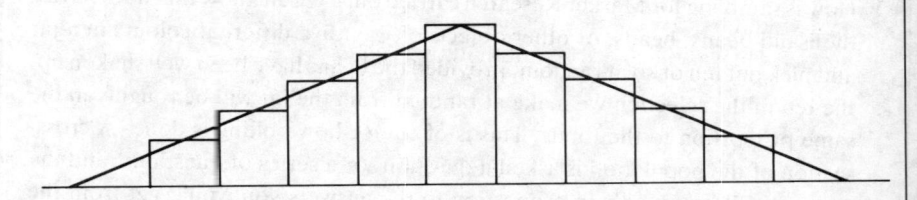

Goodness of fit

4 Experiments show that on a normal distribution curve the deviation from the mean represented by the top of the curve is equal on both sides and a 'standard deviation' can be calculated. Three standard deviations will cover about 99% of the population, only the *rogues* or *freaks* lying outside. The accuracy of the sample can be judged by doing what is called the Chi Squared test (x^2) for

'GOODNESS OF FIT', WHICH IS TO SAY A TEST OF HOW WELL THE PATTERN OF THE CURVE OF THE SAMPLE WOULD FIT A CURVE REPRESENTING THE WHOLE POPULATION.

5 We need not go into the formula here, but we can see how useful the x^2 test can be in technical or market research. Imagine we are testing the accuracy with which a machine was turning out a product that had to be within a certain *tolerance*. In our quality control we could test by sampling. Although we do not talk about goodness of performance, we do talk about quality, and when it comes to distribution curves statisticians talk about goodness of fit. Advertising men use statistics in a big way. In the 'soap war' between Proctor and Gamble and Unilever, tremendous use is made of statistics to measure the *dynamic difference* in market share resulting from the proportional allocation to advertising, which constitutes such a large part of their production costs before selling; so much so that they regard their production costs as production plus advertising costs.

It is easy to imagine circumstances in which our sampling would not throw up a normal distribution curve. If, for example, 40% of our 15-year-olds were from the Dinka tribe in the Upper Nile where adult men approach 7 feet, you would expect a lopsided curve, or, as the statisticians call it, a skew curve.

Tolerance and Dynamic difference

6 The other thing we need to understand about statistics is Probability, and how it is expressed. We know we cannot be accurate about the future. We estimate the chances. We talk about a 50% chance that something will happen which means that there is an equal chance, also 50%, that it will not happen. So .5 Probability is 50%: .9 is 90% and 100% or 1 (Unity) is Certainty. Once our crystal-ball gazers have agreed a figure with .95 probability, they can extrapolate future revenue, sales, costs, etc, on a gradient with a line 5% above it and another 5% below. They then keep *their fingers crossed* in the hope that their margin of error can be tolerated.

On one occasion a planner for Air France predicted the number of passengers that would be carried on a certain route absolutely accurately to the last passenger. He was the first to admit that it was a *fluke!*

Probability

GLOSSARY

jump in the lake	– (*coll.*) go away
tally	– mark made to register a fixed number of objects or units
rogues	– *here:* odd, wild; *usually:* rascal or swindler
freaks	– *here:* exceptions; *usually:* an abnormal example
tolerance	– *here:* margin of error; *usually:* liberty, understanding
dynamic difference	– the market share moved by the power of advertising
to keep your fingers crossed	– (*coll.*) to hope that luck will be on your side
fluke	– a lucky accident

G. Check your understanding

Now read the text carefully and say whether the following statements are correct or not.
- The answers given by a sample of the population will be quite different from what you would get if you set the questions to the whole population. ☐
- The result of a sample poll will not exactly reflect the opinion of the entire population. ☐
- The bigger the sample, the more accurate the result will be. ☐
- The size of the sample has no effect whatsoever on the result. ☐
- The persons interviewed are selected without any account of their position in the social scale. ☐
- A sample is taken from persons from the appropriate socio-economic categories. ☐
- Goodness of fit involves a comparison of the sample with the whole population. ☐
- Large companies include the cost of advertising as part of their production costs. ☐
- A probability of 0.8 means an 80% probability. ☐
- 100% probability is necessary if future trends are to be forecast. ☐

H. Understanding discourse

Listen to the talk by the Managing Director given on your tape, to see what it is all about. Then look at the following questions and play the tape again, making notes for your answers. You can expand these into full sentences later. Enter the names of the departments in both the schemes given below.

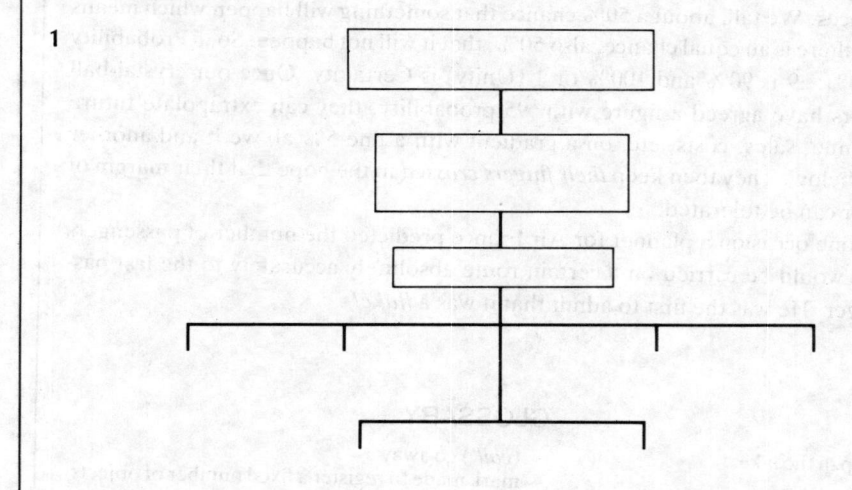

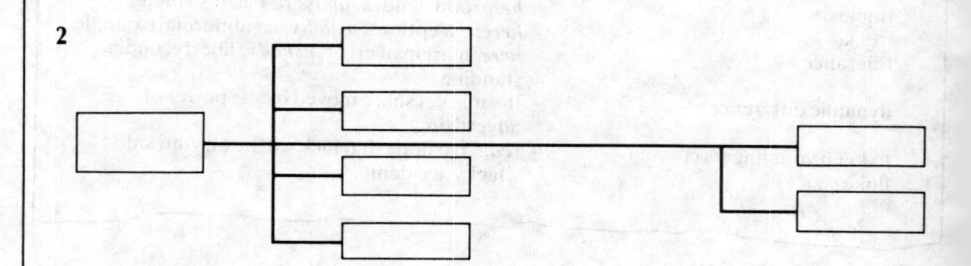

3
- Why has the MD changed the organisation of the company?
- What does he mean by '1992 and all that'?
- Who owns the company?
- How often do the shareholders meet?
- What is the significance of the order in which the MD lists the departments?
- Why has the MD provided a second variation of the new scheme?

The passages in sections A and F of this unit were taken (edited) from GILLIBRAND and MADDOCK, *The Manager and His Words*, Pergamon, 1982

CHECK YOUR PROGRESS

1

The following section is for you to check how you are acquiring the skills you will need to follow a course of Business Studies in English. It is not an examination that you must pass or fail; it is a progress check for your own information

A. Reading

You may have heard the old saying, 'Look after the pennies, and the pounds will look after themselves.' A good example of this in practice is petty cash accounting by what is called the imprest system. This is outlined in the following passage. Busy company cashiers have no time to devote to recording the expenditure of small sums ('petty' is the French word 'petit'; 'petty cash' therefore means simply 'small money') — so this is entrusted to various people in separate departments or offices. Each is given a certain sum of money (e.g., £50.00) as initial funds or 'float' for use on incidental everyday expenses. All expenditure, even of the smallest amount, must be properly accounted for. So the petty cash system is really a sort of miniature model of how a company's books are kept.

Now read the text below, which gives instructions on keeping a petty cash book. You may find it useful to look also at Figure 10.1 (on p. 46) as you read.

10.1 Keeping the petty cash (imprest system)

One of your jobs is to balance the petty cash account. You choose a time when you hope to remain undisturbed for a while, and unlock the cash box.

During the week, it is sometimes difficult to find time to enter up the petty cash book each time you make a payment, so whenever you have paid out any money you have contented yourself with placing a signed voucher in a special 5
compartment of the box. Your company provides a pad of preprinted forms for this purpose. Each voucher provides space for the amount and description of the purchase, and the signatures of the persons making and authorizing it. If a supplier's official receipt is available, you attach this to a voucher. 10

Today, you sort your vouchers into date order and number them consecutively. Taking them in numerical order, you enter in the book the date and details of each: the amount of the payment you record in the 'Total' column and repeat it in an analysis column. These column headings—cleaning, repairs and renewals, travel, postage, etc.—correspond to the titles 15
of accounts in the ledger. Where no particular column is appropriate, you use the one headed 'Sundries' (miscellaneous items). Where VAT has been paid, you enter this in the VAT column, and the price of the item concerned in the appropriate analysis column. Together they add up to the sum entered in the 'total' column. Then you insert the number of each voucher in the 20
column provided, enabling the company's cashier to check later the evidence for each entry, and then file the vouchers neatly in numerical order in a folder.

When you have entered all the items, you cast the columns, to enable each total to be posted later as a debit entry to the appropriate ledger account. 25

Then, you check that the subtotals of the analysis columns when added together equal the main 'total' column. (You have found occasionally that they do not, and then you have had to find the reason for the discrepancy. Usually carelessness in casting has caused it, a transposition in figures, or failure to note each payment in both the 'total' and an analysis column.) Next, you count up the money left in your cash box. This is your balance in hand, which when added to expenditure equals the total cash with which you started the period. (A discrepancy here could mean that some cash spent has not been accounted for. This is why you insist on receiving a voucher from anyone requiring cash, and why you never lend anyone money from the petty cash for private purposes.)

To close the account, you write in the balance in hand and insert the grand total. Level with this, on the receipts or debit side of the account you insert the corresponding total of cash in hand at the beginning of the period.

1. Now look at the statements below, and say whether you think they are correct or not by putting ticks or crosses in the boxes after them:

1. If there is no time to enter a payment in the petty cash book, you can issue a voucher instead. ☐
2. Someone has to authorise and sign each voucher. ☐
3. There is no point in adding a receipt to the voucher. ☐
4. Each amount of payment is entered in two separate places. ☐
5. The sundries column is for things that don't fit anywhere else. ☐
6. Value Added Tax (VAT) is not included in the total column. ☐
7. The subtotals need not exactly equal the figure in the total column. ☐
8. The balance of cash and total expenditure together equal the amount of the float. ☐
9. You can use petty cash to make loans to your friends. ☐
10. A petty cash account is closed by entering the cash in hand and the grand total. ☐

2. Now put a tick in the box by the correct definition of the following words as they are used in the text:

1 line **5** a *voucher* is: a receipt ☐
　　　　　　　　　　a promise to pay ☐
　　　　　　　　　　an IOU ☐
　　　　　　　　　　evidence of expenditure ☐

2 line **16**. a *ledger* is: a shelf ☐
　　　　　　　　　　a collection of accounts ☐
　　　　　　　　　　a filing cabinet ☐
　　　　　　　　　　a receipt book ☐

3 line **24** *cast* means: throw away ☐
　　　　　　　　　　　add up ☐
　　　　　　　　　　　calculate ☐
　　　　　　　　　　　subdivide ☐

4 line **25** *posted* means: transferred ☐
　　　　　　　　　　　　sent away ☐
　　　　　　　　　　　　filed ☐
　　　　　　　　　　　　put in an envelope ☐

B. Writing

Now look again closely at the extract from a petty cash book given below.

Receipts	Date	Details	Voucher	Total	VAT	Hospitality	Office sundries	Travelling	Postage
£ 60.00	May 1	Cash	Fo CB5	£	£	£	£	£	£
		Ballpoint pens	1	2.30	.30		2.00		
	" 2	String	2	1.15	.15		1.00		
	" 3	Bus fares	3	1.70				1.70	
	" 4	Stamps	4	14.00					14.00
		Coffee	5	4.14	.54	3.60			
	" 5	Typewriter ribbons	6	8.51	1.11		7.40		
				31.80	2.10	3.60	10.40	1.70	14.00
	" 5	Balance	c/d	28.20	L.81	L.23	L.79	L.28	L.26
60.00				60.00					
28.20	May 5	Balance	b/f						
31.80		Cash	Fo. CB6						

Figure 10.1 Extract from a petty cash book.

1. Write a paragraph explaining the expenditure for the period 1–5 May. Imagine that you are in charge of the account and have been asked to explain it to the chief cashier.

2. Say whether the following statements are correct or not by putting a tick or a cross in each box:

1 expenditure for the period, excluding VAT, was £31.80. ☐

2 Bus fares were not subject to payment of VAT. ☐
3 All stationery items were listed under office sundries. ☐
4 Hospitality items incur VAT. ☐
5 The cost of string, before VAT, was £1.00. ☐
6 Three bus journeys are accounted for. ☐
7 The balance on 5 May was £28.20. ☐

C. Listening

Listen to the lecture on your tape, playing it several times until you think you have mastered the contents. Then say whether the following statements are true or not by putting ticks or crosses in the boxes.

1. Accounting and bookkeeping are the same. ☐
2. An accountant is responsible for counting money. ☐
3. If you purchase on credit, you do not have to pay. ☐
4. If you supply something on credit, the purchaser can pay later. ☐
5. Purchasing on credit is advantageous to the purchaser. ☐
6. The purchaser can earn more money with the money he owes. ☐
7. The credit control department is formed to deal with bad debts. ☐
8. A bankrupt company is one that cannot pay its debts. ☐
9. If an organisation is making profits, it must be able to pay its debts. ☐
10. To open a petty cash account, you must top-up the float. ☐
11. Such a system is called impressive. ☐
12. It is not worth accounting for very small sums. ☐

> The possible score is 33.
> How did you get on? ☐

UNIT 6

DEALING WITH PEOPLE (1)

A. Understanding a printed text (1)

The following passage introduces the topic of **maintaining good communications** and relationships between managers and the people they work with. Look at the way the passage is constructed, paying especial attention to the headings and to the illustrations and captions. Then look at the following questions and read through the text quickly to find the answers. Remember that you do not have to understand every word in order to answer the questions:

1. What, in your own words, is this passage about?
2. What does Figure 1.1 show?
3. What does Figure 1.2 show?
4. What are given in Table 1.1?

HOW INFORMATION TRAVELS

Channelling information

1   Managers do not work in isolation; once they acquire information, they will often wish to pass it on. To be most effective—as we shall see—a message should be sent in the form most suited to the receiver (and that is not necessarily the form easiest for you, the sender). When you submit a recommendation to your boss you will summarize the argument as best you can, stressing the facts that support your case. When you were originally collecting the information, you may have received some items that later turn out to be irrelevant. You will not wish to waste the time of senior management with these items—it is your job to filter out the unnecessary.

Management and Communication

2   In a similar vein, when decisions are passed down to you, from on high, you will wish to 'translate' them into appropriate terms for your staff. This can sometimes take the form of receiving orders and passing on detailed instructions. The manager is thus the hub of a system of communications—a one-man communication centre (see Fig. 1.1), as well as being a powerhouse of ideas, an initiator of action, and a thinking man to boot. Information and questions come up to him; answers, decisions, and instructions go down from him. The junior manager is in the same relationship to his superiors as are his staff to him. The good manager is a good communicator—and usually, vice versa.

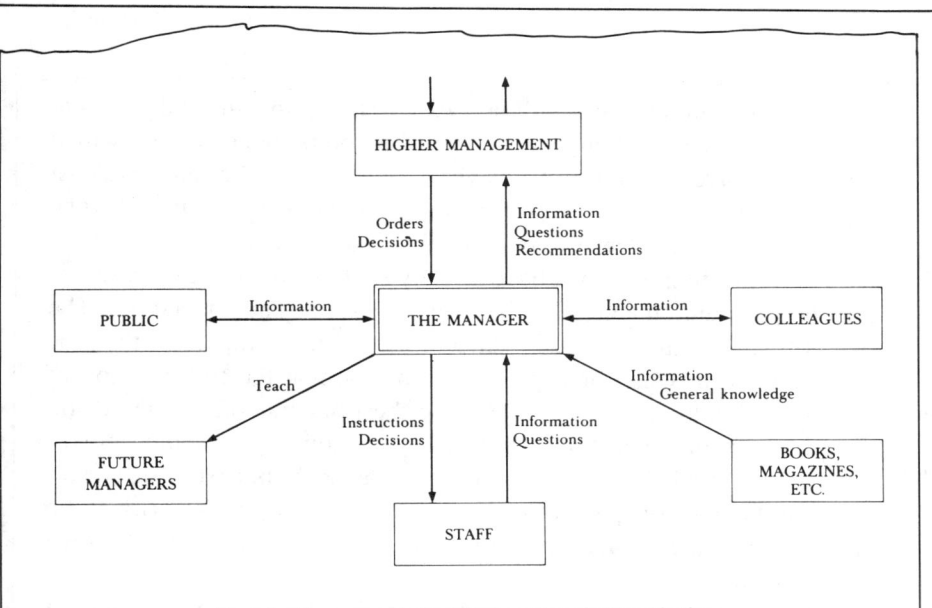

Fig. 1.1 The manager is the hub of a system of communication

3   Communications of all kinds are what make an organization work. Without adequate communications an organization will soon grind to a halt. And communications are usually intended to follow the route of the established management hierarchy (see Fig. 1.2(a)).

The formal route

4   Formal communications will, of course, pass up and down the pyramid of management as intended. What is too often forgotten is that there are other communication paths. In any organization there are inevitably social links that are unofficially and informally used to transmit 'interesting' information. ('Interesting' information can be defined as that affecting people.) The *grapevine* includes not only the social links but also everything from office gossip to post-room misinformation. Every office, every factory, every organization, has its grapevine (see Fig. 1.2(b)).

The grapevine

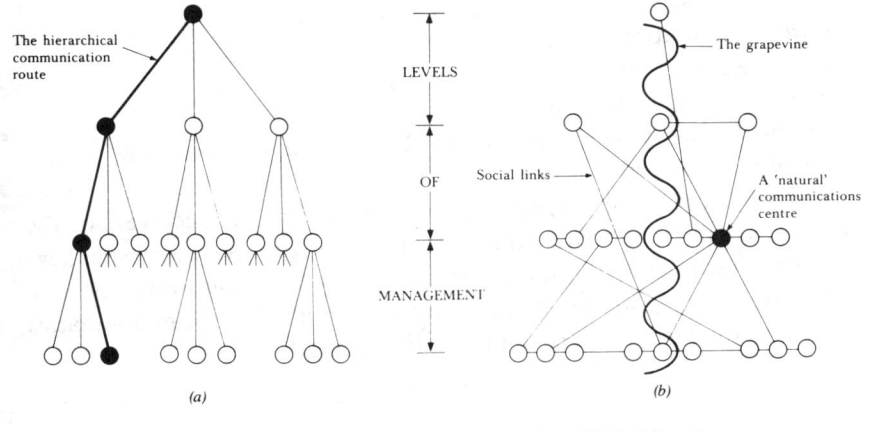

Fig. 1.2 Two communication systems: (a) the formal, and (b) the informal

Two-way communication

The good communicator will be aware of the grapevine and plug into it. Not all that he obtains from it will be complimentary, nor will it always be correct, but it will always be interesting and often useful. At times the manager can feed information into the grapevine himself. If he is not to lose all credence though, his input must always be correct.

5   Communication is, as we have already said, a two-way process. It is not complete until the message has been received—and understood. The extent to which the message is understood is more important than the way or form in which it is sent. This means that the transmission of messages should always be in the form best understood by the person receiving them. Some things are best said, some best written down. Throughout this book that principle is repeated: think first, last, and all the time about the recipient or audience or reader. Adjust the writing, the speaking, and the arithmetic to suit him. And if pictures will help, give him a picture.

Clearly, the style and quality of communication will depend not just on the sender and the receiver but also on their relationship to each other. A small, informal, organization will suggest a different style of communication to a large, rigidly-controlled, hierarchical one. In all cases it is necessary to select the best mode for communication.

Methods of communication

Communication modes

6   Animals communicate with barks, whinnies and snarls. It is man's ability to transmit more complex messages by a variety of modes that, among other things, separates him from the animals. Fundamentally, however, man communicates only by sight or by sound, but within those categories, there are others. Moving rapidly away from the realms of sociology into the mundane world of management, we can define a manager's communication modes as:

verbal—the written word
oral—the spoken word
visual—the illustration, and
numerical—the written—and interpreted—number; and now
electronic—using a computer.

Further, within the above categories, there are the receivers of the messages. For every writer, there must be a reader, for every speaker a listener, and for every artist a viewer. Communication in numbers is perhaps new to some, but to the managers with a feel for mathematics, numbers too can be easily read and interpreted.

7   We have explained that a communication is not made until it is received and understood. The prime essential in any form of communication is therefore to know the audience. It is important also to accept the concept that people tend to receive —to hear, to read, to see—very largely only what they want to receive. They seek out what is expected and what is familiar while trying to ignore or reject what is new. Every communication should be made with that thought in mind. The answer is, of course, to ensure that every message is clear, simple and—as far as possible—unambiguous. However, no matter how much the sender of the message may try, the taking of that message depends on the past experience (the training) of the recipient. This characteristic can also be partially allowed for in the communication process—by departing from the well known and moving in short, simple steps towards the really new.

When does communication take place?

8   Throughout the previous paragraph there is an implied message that is too often ignored and is worth emphasizing. This is that for any communication to be worth while, it must have a purpose—and that purpose is always *persuasion*. This is not to say that there are no purposeless communications: there are too many, but they are usually of little value to anyone. Every genuine communication seeks to influence the recipient. It may seek to persuade him to take some course of action, to make a decision one way or another, or merely to apply his mind to accepting more information. If we think about persuasion it is clear that we are most likely to succeed if acceptance of the persuasion is made easy.

The purpose of communication

9   We have therefore identified the fundamental principle of communication as: *transmit all communications in the manner best suited to the recipient's understanding*. This rather ponderous phrase could itself be better communicated as: *write (or speak) clearly and simply so that the reader (or listener) can easily understand* (see Table 1.1).

Table 1.1 Do unto others as you would be done by

1. Communicate only when you have something worth while to say.
2. Don't write or speak at greater length than is necessary to convey the message.
3. Write in such a way that the reader will find it easy to read.
4. Read carefully, concentrating on absorbing and understanding the writer's message.
5. Speak in 'the language' of your listeners—but never talk down.
6. Listen attentively to a speaker and avoid mind-wandering.
7. Help an interview candidate to feel at ease; encourage him to speak.
8. Where helpful, supplement words with pictures.
9. Watch speakers and listeners for 'non-verbal' signals.
10. Explain mathematical information with summaries, words and pictures.

B. Check your understanding

1. Read through the text carefully, looking up anything you do not understand. Then answer the following questions:

1. In what form should a message ideally be sent?
2. Why should you summarise your argument in order to present a recommendation?
3. How can you save the time of senior management?
4. What must a manager do, as well as thinking and initiating actions?
5. What happens to organisations in which communications are poor?
6. Are formal communications the only route by which information spreads?
7. How is 'interesting' information defined?
8. Is such information always complimentary to the manager?
9. After a message has been sent, what is still required before communication may be said to have taken place?
10. Is it best always to write things down?
11. On what factors do the style of communication depend?
12. Name the five modes of communication used by man.
13. What is the prime need if communication is to be effective?

14. What do people tend to read or hear?
15. What is the essential purpose of any communication?
16. What should therefore be done in order to make a communication acceptable?
17. When should you communicate?
18. How should you write?
19. Should one talk down to one's listener?
20. When should pictures be used?

2. Look at Figure 1.1 and answer the following questions:
- Where does a manager receive information from?
- To whom does he pass it?
- What is the information flow between manager and public?
- Which system of communication does Figure 1.1 refer to?

C. Increase your vocabulary

1. Rephrase in your own words the following expressions taken from the text:

paragraph 1, line 3: (the form) most suited to the receiver
              6: as best you can

paragraph 2, line 1:   in a similar vein
              lines 1–2: from on high
              lines 6–7: (and a thinking man) to boot
              line 10:   (and usually) vice versa

paragraph 3, lines 2–3: (an organization will soon) grind to a halt

paragraph 4, lines 13–14: (if he is not) to lose all credence

paragraph 6, lines 5–6: the realms (of sociology)
              line 6:   the mundane world (of management)

paragraph 9, line 3: this rather ponderous phrase

2. Look at Table 1.1 and explain what is meant by the forms in italics:
rule 1: something *worth while* to say
rule 2: *at greater length* than is necessary
rule 5: never *talk down*
rule 6: avoid *mind-wandering*
rule 9: *non-verbal* signals

D. Check your grammar

In the following references to the passage, say what the words indicated refer to:

- paragraph 1, line 2: it
             4: that
             9: these (items)

- paragraph 2, line 2: them
             3: this

- paragraph 4, line 8: its
             11: it, it

- paragraph 5, line 1: it
             4: it
             9: him
             12: their

E. Understanding a lecture

Listen to the lecture about body language on your tape, playing it through as many times as necessary for you to understand it all. Look at the questions below, and play the tape section by section, making notes for your answers. Then write a summary of the main points in the lecture.

1.
   - What is the main medium of communication between people?
   - What additional means of communication is there? Give both its names.
   - If an Englishman does not agree with what you are saying, what will he probably do?
   - If you disagreed with him, what would you do?
   - Is a smile always a signal of pleasure?
   - Why is an awareness of NVC important to managers?
   - What are the five commonly quoted categories of NVC?
   - What does an American mean by 'invasion of his space'?
   - If I were twisting a handkerchief in my fingers all the time I was talking to you, what would this signify?
   - Can body language be learned?

2. Note down the NVC signals you receive during your next conversation with someone. Then try to remember what signals you yourself gave. Write an analysis of what you think they meant.

F. Understanding a printed text (2)

HUMAN BEHAVIOUR (1)

1   Why do people behave the way they do in organizations? Why do some work so hard while others appear to do the minimum required? Why do two people have such different rates of productivity? Why do some like highly structured jobs while others want freedom and autonomy? What makes some satisfied and happy while others seem unhappy? Why do some work alone and others spend all their time in groups? Why are some people money-hungry while others are almost unaffected by monetary rewards? It is questions like these that managers want answered.

2   It is not very helpful to managers to be told simply that people are different. They know that already. What managers find useful are reference points against which they can map data about the individuals they have to manage. People drop clues all the time about their experiences, goals and expectations. One function of a manager is to collect those clues and use them to discover the abilities, goals, events, etc., that are important to that individual. Once they know what is important to the individual employee, managers then have the key to motivating that person for better performance. They have to link the individual's goals to those of the organization.

3   One of our objectives, as managers, is to attempt to predict future performances. To help elucidate this extremely complex process I will look at five major influences on how an individual behaves at work:

- Abilities
- Experience
- Goals and values
- Energy
- Expected rewards

If individuals have the necessary abilities and experience and their goals are the same as those of the organization, then, provided they find the rewards attractive and have the energy, they will work hard to achieve those goals.

Let us examine each of these factors.

Why do people behave as they do?

Matching goals

Predicting performance

4 Abilities

From a very early age we learn (despite parental reassurances) that some people are much better at, say, drawing or running or language than we are. For this reason abilities have attracted a great deal of attention as we attempt to devise ways of assessing their levels in individuals. Schools, colleges and universities and business organizations measure abilities religiously and, on the basis of test results, attempt to predict an individual's future performance.

Unfortunately the relationship between performance and both formal and informal assessments of abilities is a disappointing one. Ability clearly does influence performance: some people undeniably have the ability to be better at some jobs than the majority of the population. However, knowing the abilities of a person only tells us that there is potential; it is another piece of data to add to our file. Ability is not a good predictor of performance in work organizations; knowing someone has the ability will not permit a manager to predict performance.

5 Experience

An experienced employee will outperform the novice. Temporary staff suffer inordinately from a lack of experience within the organization—experience of its systems, structure, strategies, etc. (by experience we mean knowledge, skills and practice, and situational familiarity). Performance will increase with experience wherever knowledge, skill and practice are relevant to the job. Performance also increases if an individual 'knows the scene'. However, we cannot predict people's actual performance from their level of experience. It may contribute to performance but it is, like ability, merely a guide to potential. The practical advantage of experience is the effect it has on confidence. Knowing that one can do the job provides an excellent foundation.

G. Check your understanding

1. Read the text carefully and say whether the following statements are, in the author's opinion, correct or not:
- Everyone in an organisation works equally hard. ☐
- All members of an organisation have equal rates of productivity. ☐
- Some like highly structured jobs, but others do not. ☐
- Some prefer not to be in a group. ☐
- Everyone wants more money. ☐
- The manager has to relate what a worker wants to what the organisation wants. ☐
- It is not a manager's job to make predictions about performance. ☐
- People who have the necessary skills, experience and goals will naturally work hard. ☐
- Some people are better at languages than others. ☐
- One can predict other people's performance if one knows what experience they have. ☐

2. Explain in your own words the meaning of the following extracts as they are used in the text:

- paragraph 1, line 8: unaffected by monetary rewards

- paragraph 2, line 3: reference points against which they can map data

- paragraph 3, line 2: to help elucidate this extremely complex process

- paragraph 4, line 1: despite parental reassurances
                  4: to devise ways of assessing their levels
                  6: measure abilities religiously

- paragraph 5, lines 1–2: temporary staff suffer inordinately
           line 4:   situational familiarity
                 7:   knows the scene
                 9:   a guide to potential

H. Understanding discourse

On your tape you will hear a tutor talking about office design, that is, about the layout of offices in a building. Listen to the tape to find what it is all about, then look at the plan below and write in the names of the offices as given on the tape. Then answer the questions given on the next page.

A conventional office building

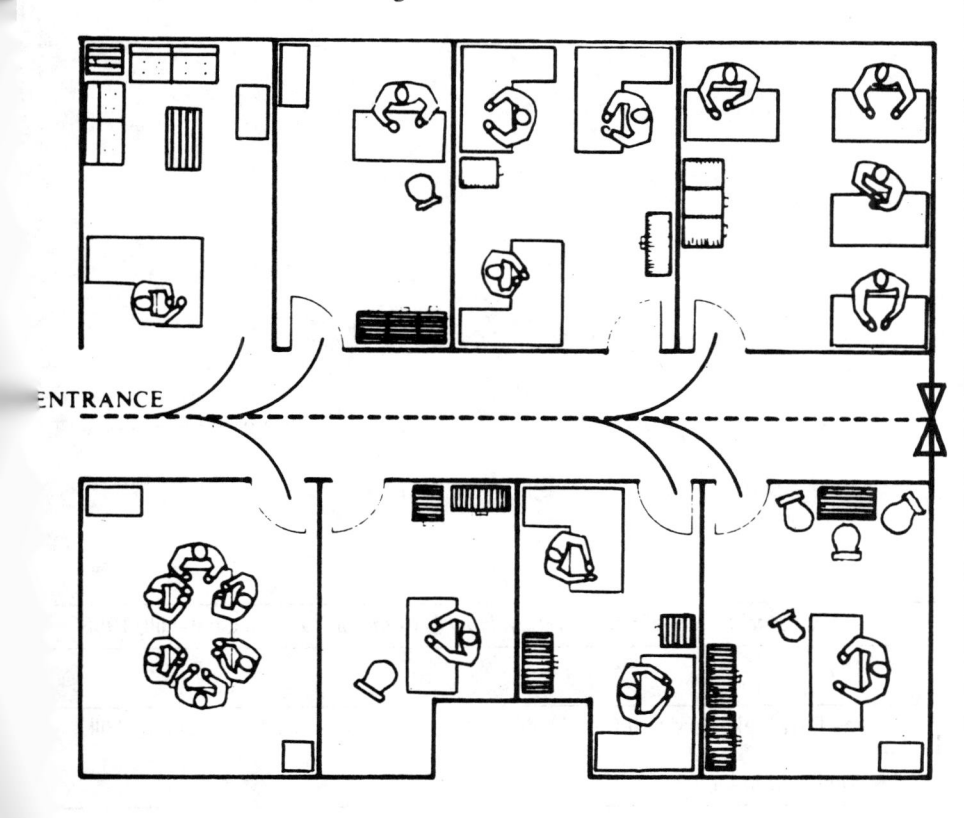

1. What does a receptionist do?
2. Where is the General Office?
3. Where does the Director's secretary sit?
4. Who shares her office?
5. Where is the Conference Room?
6. What is the main item of furniture in it?
7. What is on the other side of the corridor from the Sales Office?
8. What is the advantage for the Director of this sort of arrangement?
9. What is the technical name for it?
10. Why?

Passage A was taken (edited) from WELLS, *How to Communicate*, McGraw-Hill, 1986

Passage F was taken (edited) from HUNT, *Managing People at Work*. McGraw-Hill, 1979.
It is continued in Unit 7.

DEALING WITH PEOPLE (2)

UNIT 7

A. Understanding a printed text (1)

The following passage continues the topic introduced in Unit 6A. Look at the way it is constructed, paying special attention to the margin notes and headings and to the illustration and caption. Then look at the following questions and read through the text quickly to find the answers. Remember, you do not have to understand every word in order to answer the questions.

1. What is the topic of this passage?
2. What main modes of communication are discussed?
3. What two simple rules does the author recommend?
4. What does Figure 2.1 illustrate?

COMMUNICATION MODES

1 *The written word*

The first major communication mode is the written word. In writing, the primary rule is to keep everything short and simple: the words, the sentences, and the ideas. It is never right to try to impress, it either appears patronizing or else just silly. Too many aspiring managers seem to feel a need to pepper their prose with long, little-understood words. ('Surely it *looks better*', that is, impresses, 'if I write "serendipitously" rather than "by chance"?'—to quote a particularly bad, but real-life, example.) If everyone wrote the way they spoke, management reports would be brighter and probably clearer, even though they would sometimes be less polite or less grammatical. Simple punctuation too should be the aim: good punctuation aids understanding, incorrect punctuation usually makes bad writing worse.

Keep it simple

Given clearer and simpler writing, the manager will be able to read faster and more profitably. We all have too much to read. If we can learn to read better, our lives become easier and our decisions potentially wiser, because our information will be more complete. Better reading comes with concentration—and practice.

One of the fundamental aids to effective reading is the making of notes. These can either be in the form of questions arising from the writer's words (which we hope to have answered as we read on) or just a picking out of the main points of an argument. Notes can, with advantage, be made on the page itself. There is no need to keep books or reports in pristine condition. They are of greater use when annotated. So, no one should hesitate before writing on their own copies of any book or report.

59

2 The spoken word

The other main communication mode is the spoken word. Most of us find little difficulty in talking to each other. It is only when talking becomes 'speaking' that it becomes difficult. But speaking in public is unnecessarily feared. As long as we recognize the large amount of preparation needed and have something to say, these fears can be allayed.

Keep it natural

Anyone can learn to speak at least adequately in public. To be a brilliant speaker is a bigger problem: it may well entail a particular flair. The best way of getting a message across in speech is to be natural; not to read a script, but to speak just from notes. 'Thinking on the feet' is the recommended approach, but to speak without any notes at all is folly. A speaker must watch his audience—a thing no writer can do—and adjust the presentation of his message to the visible reactions of the audience.

We have already remarked that it takes two to communicate. Just as a writer needs a reader, so too does each speaker require a listener. We can all improve on our listening skills and the most important part of listening is to concentrate. Because the brain can work significantly faster than a person can speak, listening is conducive to mind-wandering. A wandering brain soon falls asleep. The recommended anti-sleep precaution is to summarize the speaker's argument as he progresses, noting it down for future reference and formulating questions that you hope the speaker will eventually answer. As memory is often short lived, and/or unreliable, a brief written note of any important message will pay dividends.

Interviews

Interviews and committee meetings necessitate the use of most of the skills of communication. Before a meeting or an interview, the wise man reads all of the necessary background papers and other material. His object is to be better equipped, mentally, for the encounter than the other participant(s). Adequately prepared, he can then attend the meeting or interview confident of his understanding of the position. He can devote all his 'mind-time' to the problem or the candidate. Throughout every meeting or interview, the good manager again makes notes; he does not rely on others' notes or on the eventual arrival of the formal minutes. After the meeting or interview it is always worth writing up scribbled personal notes into a legible and permanent record.

3 *Other modes*

But written and spoken words, although the main modes of management communication, are not the only ones. We all know how a newspaper picture can often speak louder and clearer than any commentary. So too can something difficult for a manager to express in words often easily be made clear with a simple diagram. To a numerate manager—accountant, economist, engineer or scientist—numbers often express concepts more clearly than words. However, the numerate man is usually less good than he should be at explaining the meaning of these numbers. There are some simple ways of using and explaining numbers, which can readily be learnt.

Visual communication for management does not have to be very artistic—the ability to rule a straight line will take you a long way. Most management illustrations are simple diagrams, but visual communication is not confined to pictures and graphs. People themselves transmit visual messages the whole time, often unwittingly: our eyes widen, we lean forward—both signals denoting an increased interest. The good manager notices such signals and takes advantage of them. Other signals—to display confidence or well-being—can be deliberately adopted to create a desired impression.

Visuals

Numbers

Body language

4 **Think first**

By working at the techniques recommended in this book, most aspiring managers will considerably improve their ability to communicate. One recommendation that cannot be repeated too often is to *think first*.

Before sending any message the sender needs to think to:

- confirm that there is a *need* to communicate;
- determine *to whom* the message is to be sent;
- clarify the *objective* of the message; and
- clarify the *content* of the message.

Finally, as a spur to diligence in studying the techniques described hereafter, remember that better communication will help *you*.

5 **Summary**

1. Communication entails the passing of a message from one person to another. It takes two to communicate—a sender and a receiver. Sending alone is not communicating.
2. Management includes anyone in authority over another. Many people can therefore be said to be involved in management.

3. Managers depend on information, which has to be communicated to them. They then pass on selected items to other managers. Every manager is the centre of a communication system.
4. In most organizations there are two communication networks: the formal office hierarchy and the grapevine. The good communicator makes use of both.
5. Communication techniques can be looked at as falling into four main classes: the written word, the spoken word, the illustration, and the written number. Within each of these classes there are two modes—the sender and the receiver.
6. The fundamental principle applicable to all active communication modes is to communicate clearly and simply in such a way that the message can readily be understood by the recipient.
7. Before initiating any communication, think. Determine the need, the recipient, the objective, and the content of each communication.

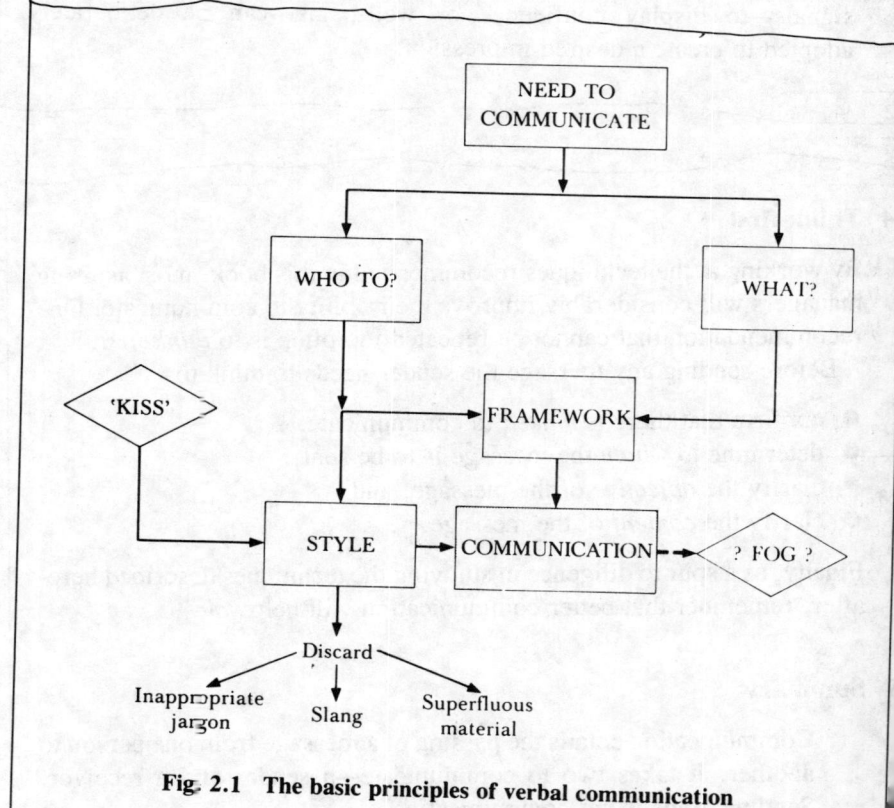

Fig. 2.1 The basic principles of verbal communication

B. Check your understanding

1. Read the passage through carefully, looking up anything you do not understand. Then answer the following questions:

1. What is the primary rule in writing?
2. Should the writer set out to impress?
3. What effect would it have if people wrote the way they spoke?
4. What sort of punctuation should be used?
5. If writing is clear and simple, what effect will this have on reading?
6. Does making notes help to make reading more effective?
7. Should one be afraid of speaking in public?
8. Should a public speaker read from notes?
9. Why should a speaker watch his audience?
10. What is the most important part of listening?
11. Why is it that when you are listening to a speech, your mind may begin to wander?
12. What is the recommended way to prevent this?
13. Why would making brief notes of important points be of value?
14. What is the usual function of a diagram?
15. If a listener's eyes widen, what does this signify?

2. Look at Figure 2.1 and say:
- What is meant by the box marked FOG?
- What is jargon?
- What is slang?

C. Increase your vocabulary

Explain what is meant by the following words and expressions in the context of the passage you have read:

- paragraph 1, line 4: patronizing
  aspiring
  5: to pepper their prose
  23: pristine condition

  paragraph 2, lines 5–6: fears can be allayed
  8: a particular flair
  9: getting a message across
  10: thinking on the feet
  11: folly
  13: visible reactions

- paragraph 2, lines 18–19: listening is conducive to mind-wandering
  - 20: anti-sleep precaution
  - 21: for future reference
  - 24: will pay dividends

- paragraph 3, lines 2–3: a newspaper picture can often speak louder and clearer than any commentary
  - 5: numerate manager
  - 15: often unwittingly

- paragraph 4: line 9: as a spur to diligence

- Figure 2.1: superfluous material

D. Check your grammar

> **Remember**
> It is never right to try to impress the audience.
> Trying to impress the audience is never right.

Now write out the following examples in both forms:
- The primary rule is to keep everything short.
- One of the fundamental aids is to make notes.
- The other way to communicate is to use the spoken word.
- One recommendation that cannot be repeated too often is to think first.
- The fundamental principle is to communicate clearly.
- Staying awake is a great problem in a dull lecture.
- Saying what you mean clearly and briefly is quite difficult.
- Thinking what you are saying is just as important as saying it well.

E. Understanding a lecture

Play the lecture on your tape in order to get an impression of what it contains. Then look at the following questions, play the tape again section by section, and make notes for your answers. Then write the answers as a summary of the lecture.

Section 1
- What does KISS mean?
- What does the KISS rule refer to?

Section 2
- What does it say about the length of sentences?
- What does it say about paragraphs?
- What sort of reports does it recommend?

Section 3
- How many sentences of average length would you expect to find in an average paragraph according to the KISS formula?

Section 4
- Why should you vary the length of paragraphs?
- When are two words better than one?
- How would you suggest urgency in your writing?

Section 5
- How much punctuation should you use?

Section 6
- Why is an exclamation mark sometimes called a 'screech mark'?
- Is developing a clear style easy to do?
- What did the writer mean when he said that he did not have time to write a shorter letter?

F. Understanding a printed text (2)

HUMAN BEHAVIOUR (2)

1   While abilities and experience give us clues about current, and possibly future, performance, the most useful information comes from an individual's goals and the values and beliefs they represent.

Motivation results from arousal and choice in the individual—a desire to allocate time and energy to a particular goal in exchange for some expected result or reward. More generally, motivation is the degree to which an individual chooses to engage in certain behaviours. This involves:

- Goals
- Arousal
- Choice
- Persistence

The most popular arousal theories with managers have been need theories. These theories collect goals, aspirations, values and behaviour into motives and call them drives, wants or needs, as though each need is a psychological construct buried in the individual's head and capable of independent analysis.

Goals and values

Energy

2   We have looked at abilities, experience and goals as they might influence behaviour at work. The fourth variable is energy, and there are two issues here. Deciding—consciously or not—to expend energy involves a choice *and* an assessment of the total energy available. Some people simply have more energy than others, while others decide to put a higher *proportion* of their energy into their careers.

Why is it that some people have more energy to give to their careers than others? Like all other factors we have discussed, energy is not easily isolated from goals, rewards, abilities, etc. However, any observer will note that the energy some people are prepared to expend in pursuing organizational goals varies greatly. Yet we tend to assume it is equal in all people. Further, we have difficulties isolating energy from social approval. Are people who work till 10 o'clock of an evening more energetic than those who stop at 5 o'clock? Perhaps the former are slower; or perhaps they are doing it because they want people to say they are working hard.

Assessing overall energy levels in people can be a relatively simple matter. Clues are:

- Activity rate.
- Numbers of hours of activity.
- Hours of rest (sleep).
- Choice of and participation in leisure and sporting activities.

Those people who seem to spend their entire lives in a state of hyperactivity provide a selection interviewer with plenty of information. For example, they seem to survive on a few hours' sleep; they will report waking and getting up early (often to the annoyance of their families); sporting activities include frenetic games (squash) and/or strenuous single-person sports (running, swimming). They will, conversely, be disparaging about inactivity; for example, watching the television is a 'waste of time'. This theme of energy or stamina reappears in their careers as a determination not to go under when the ship hits a storm, a striving to avoid failure.

Beyond these fairly obvious signs, the interviewer has problems. Many people take their careers extremely seriously because it is the only way for them to establish who and what they are. Indeed, the whole of the Western economic system depends on a strong link between personal identity and job, although there are significant cultural differences between the newer societies (the USA, Australia) and the older (the UK, France, Holland). If individuals do not need a job or title or status to know who they are (e.g., in older societies), then the energy they put into their job or career may seem slight to those in the new societies. Yet these same people may have great sources of energy which are only seen in non-career activity.

Guilt also plays a part in the energy expended. If child-rearing practices include guilt and a strong work ethic, then the probability that energy will be expended in work tends to increase. Indeed, the popular myth that the work ethic (by which people mean an emphasis on hard-working, persistent and conscientious behaviour) is dead is *not* supported by research. Work, if not career, remains the primary goal of individuals.

Expected rewards

3 Organizations offer the individual inducements to work and to work hard. These inducements are both extrinsic and intrinsic.

- *Extrinsic rewards* Those tangible rewards that probably attract most of us into the workforce in the first place. Indeed, they provide a more likely explanation for the level of employment than the work ethic—i.e., necessity is the motivator. Extrinsic rewards include wages, salary, bonuses, commission payments, working conditions, a car, pension, etc.
- *Intrinsic rewards* The goal satisfactions of working—lifestyle, comfort, a sense of achievement, companionship, status, public acclaim, challenge, interesting tasks, etc. These rewards of work are often referred to collectively as job satisfaction.

It is sufficient here to recognize that individuals at work are motivated by the sorts of rewards that are available. Thereafter it is a choice as to whether, with their abilities, experience, goals and energy levels, they will choose to work.

G. Check your understanding

Read through the passage carefully, looking up anything you do not undersand. Then say if the following statements are true or not true?

- Motivation comes from arousal and choice. ☐
- An individual who works towards a specific goal will expect to receive something in exchange. ☐
- Wants and needs are the same thing. ☐
- Some people expend more energy on building a career than others do. ☐
- It is correct to assume that all people have equal amounts of energy to expend on organisational goals. ☐
- People may work longer hours just to create the impression that they are working harder. ☐
- Hyperactive people may consider watching television to be a waste of time. ☐
- There is not much cultural difference between the USA and France. ☐
- The most important goal for most people is work. ☐
- What attracts most people to work is the expectation of reward. ☐

H. Understanding discourse

On your tape you will hear the tutor talking again about the layout of offices, this time according to an open plan system. Listen to the tape to find what it is all about, then look at the plan below and write in the names of the positions given on the tape. Then answer the questions given underneath.

An open plan office

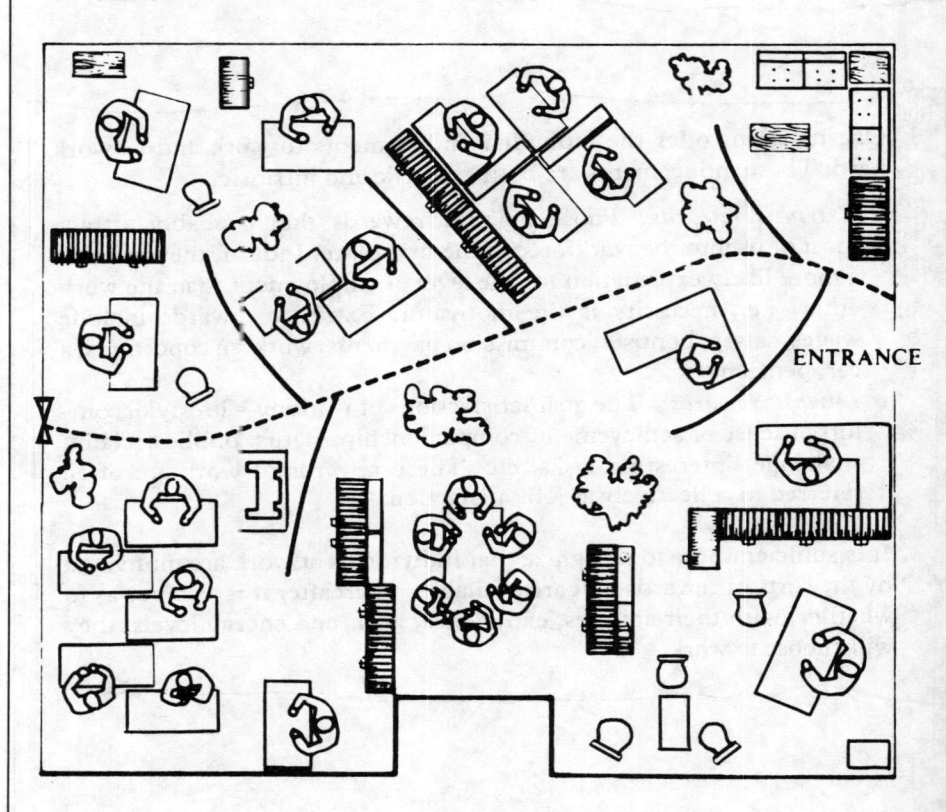

1. What is the main difference between an open plan office and a cellular one?
2. What separates the typing pool from the waiting area on your plan?
3. Where does the Sales Manager sit?
4. Is there a central corridor?
5. Where does the Receptionist sit?
6. What is the effect of the potted shrubs?
7. What lessens the noise in a modern office?
8. What effect does the open plan style have on control of the atmosphere?
9. How can the different treatment of senior staff be preserved?
10. Are open plan offices common?

Passage A was taken (edited) from WELLS, *How to Communicate*, McGraw-Hill, 1986

Passage F was taken (edited) from HUNT, *Managing People at Work*. McGraw-Hill, 1979

MANAGING THE PAPERWORK

UNIT 8

A. Understanding a printed text (1)

The passage introduces the topic of dealing efficiently with the **reading and writing** tasks of the business manager. Look at the way it is constructed, especially the headings, margin notes, illustration and caption. Then look at the following questions and read through the text quickly to find the answers. Remember, you do not have to understand every word in order to answer the questions:

1. Which task does passage A deal with?
2. What main purposes of reading does it isolate?
3. How does it suggest a manager tackles the problem?
4. What does Figure 4.1 show?

A. READING

1 Every manager has too much to read. Paper flows across the managerial desk in a continuous stream. It cannot be ignored; it keeps coming in and if not dealt with, will assuredly fill the room. As already remarked, for every manager who writes a letter or report, there is a presupposed reader—and it is always *you*. Reading is the passive component of page-bound communication. It is also one of the means whereby a manager keeps in touch with what is going on. Without this awareness he cannot manage. There is therefore a need to learn how to cope—how to read efficiently.

The need to read

2 Most managers' reading material consists of the following:

- letters, requiring response or passing on, up or down;
- copies of the letters of others and the 'float', or 'daily carbons';
- reports, minutes, or brief notes of past meetings, for information and/or for check;
- advice (agenda and 'papers') of future meetings;
- reports needing attention, decision, or comment; and
- trade journals, often with only minimal direct relevance.

To the above list, the aspiring manager would no doubt add a few textbooks—in management methods or a specialist discipline—and some leisure reading, newspapers, novels, etc. The manager will also, of course, be expected to check the typing of his own writing—for errors, changes of mind, etc.

Reading material

These last two aspects of management reading are outside the context of this particular exercise. The checking of typescript requires careful attention, but it is largely a mechanical process, entailing no fresh interpretation. Leisure reading is important to any manager, but our only suggestion is that the aspiring manager choose well-written novels rather than trash.

3 Purposes

Why read?

With the exception of type-checking and leisure reading, management reading can be thought of as serving three main purposes. These are:

- reading for action;
- reading for information; and
- reading for learning.

It is important to be clear for which purpose one is reading. Different purposes require different approaches.

Reading for action

4   Within the broad purpose of reading for action fall the letters requiring answer, the recommendations and reports requiring decisions, and—to varying extent—the papers for forthcoming meetings. Most of these papers will need to be read carefully, and completely. But before reading them, the appropriate documents must be selected; the wheat that has to be processed, separated from the chaff which is best left or passed to others.

Reading for information

5   Reading for information covers all the papers directly connected with day-to-day work but not requiring decision. Included in this category are obviously such things as the 'daily carbons', other people's letters that may occasionally have a bearing on your own work, and reports of other people's meetings. All the material needs to be looked at—but usually only as background, or defensive, information.

Reading for learning

6   The third purpose, reading for learning, relates particularly to trade journals and to possible textbooks. It comprises that reading which is done to improve one's overall professional knowledge and managerial efficiency. A vast amount of such material is available and much of it crosses the managerial desk. The overwhelming need here is to *select* which feature, article, or textbook ought to be read and which can safely be discarded. Once that choice is made, the approach should be as detailed and careful as when reading for action.

7   In order to use your reading time efficiently, it is worth developing a systematic approach. For this, the most important requirement is concentration. To read efficiently—without daydreaming, at as fast a pace as is compatible with adequate understanding—requires the reader's undivided attention. If you find yourself not aware of what you are reading (and it happens to all of us), stop a while and do something as different as possible: stretch your legs, walk across the room and back, then start again, mentally refreshed. It is often worth while breaking up your reading time into thirty-minute stints, with two- or three-minute gaps between them. Reading without concentration will waste far more time than these frequent deliberate breaks. And remember, nothing looks worse than a manager who actually falls asleep, even if he is reading a dull report.

A systematic approach

The two basic inputs to a reading process are therefore an awareness of your purpose (why are you reading?) and a willingness and ability to concentrate.

8 A management reading process

Within the three reading purposes mentioned above there is a need:

- to sift through, to select for more careful reading;
- to read fairly quickly, to obtain a general idea; and/or
- to read some material very carefully (see Fig. 4.1).

Sorting the material

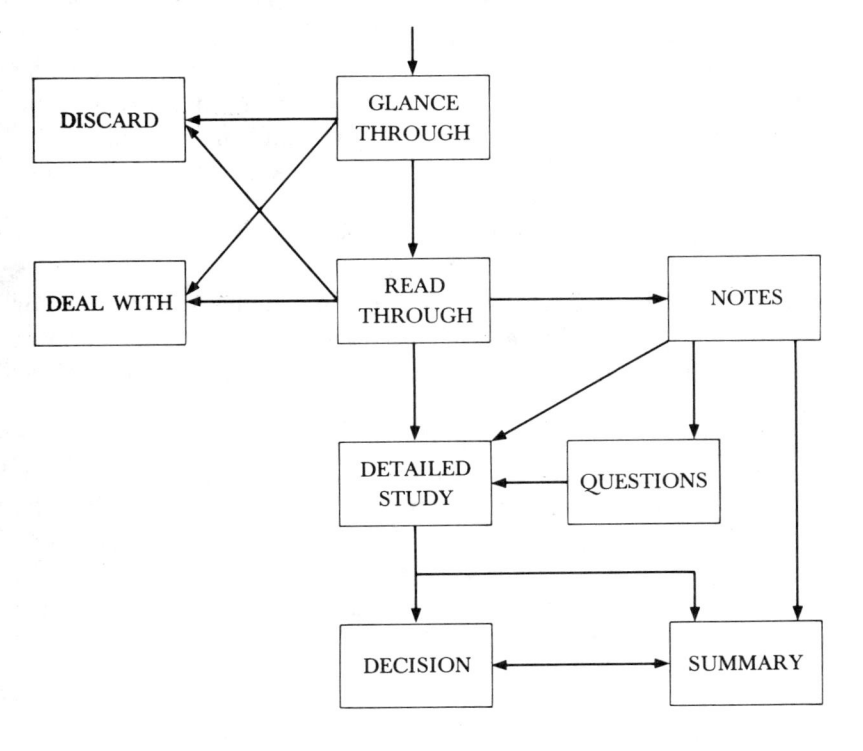

Fig. 4.1 A management reading process

9   Visualize your in-tray after two or three days out of the office. It may well be piled high—depending on the existence and ability of a secretary or aide—and you have to deal with it. If you are human (and who isn't?) you will never just start at the top and work steadily down through the pile; nor should you. The normal—and correct—approach is to glance at everything, getting a rough idea of what confronts you. That way you can sort out the boss's and other 'immediate' notes from the two-day-old advertising material or 'puff' mail.

Extend that process—after you have pacified the boss and dealt with anything legitimately tagged as immediate. Not all of the contents of the tray will need to remain with you. Those that do need not all be treated in the same way, they will need to be read for different purposes. Clearly the papers needing to be read for personal action will take pride of place; others can be deferred.

Look first at letters specifically addressed or referred to you. In many cases the letter-head itself will suggest what needs to be done, ranging from waste-paper basket to immediate deferential response. Glance too at the subject heading. If the letter is short, read it right through and decide on the action necessary. If it is a long letter—two or three pages—read the first and last paragraph carefully, and glance at the rest. That, together with knowledge of the subject and the sender, will usually give an adequate initial idea of its content—a 'feel'. It will help you to decide whether to pass it on or deal with it yourself, and when.

Look next at reports, 'copies for information', papers for forthcoming meetings, etc. Often there will be a covering note saying what you are expected to do: 'decision by Friday', 'for information only', etc. Beyond this, within each report or paper, look at the title, the sub-headings in the text, any illustrations, and the summary. (If there is no formal summary, try the final paragraph or two.) This quick look will usually suffice to give you a 'feel' of the contents, to help you to decide what to do with it. Treat letters copied to you (whether specifically 'for information' or on a 'daily carbon' system) in a similar way to your own letters. Glance through them, noting sender, addressee and subject. Most will not affect you. The one or two that do, of course, read carefully. Pass on, discard or file all others—quickly.

Finally, those trade journals. Look first at the contents page. From this any potentially interesting feature articles can be identified. The article itself will almost certainly have some sort of 'blurb' at its head—elaborating on the title—which will suffice to confirm its interest. Papers in more learned technical journals will usually have a brief abstract serving the same purpose.

B. Check your understanding

Re-read the passage carefully, looking up anything you do not understand. Then answer the following questions.

1. Can a manager safely ignore the reading matter that arrives on his desk?
2. What is presupposed whenever anything is written?
3. What is likely to happen if a manager loses touch with what is going on around him?
4. What action does he take when he receives a letter?
5. Why does he receive minutes of past meetings?
6. Who checks his typed letters?
7. Does checking a typescript require great thought?
8. Does it matter what a manager reads in his spare time?
9. How should one treat papers for forthcoming meetings?
10. What is the point of reading copies of other people's letters?
11. How would you define 'reading for learning'?
12. On what basis should you select what to read?
13. Why is it useful to develop a systematic approach to reading?
14. What is the most important element in reading?
15. What would you do if you found it difficult to concentrate on something you were reading?
16. What other factor is important in reading, as well as concentration?
17. If your in-tray is full, should you start at the top and work right through it?
18. How should you first treat a long letter?
19. What is the first thing you should look at in a report?
20. Why should you begin reading a journal by looking at the contents page?

C. Increase your vocabulary

1. Explain in your own words the meaning of the following expressions as they are used in the text:

- paragraph 1, line 5:   passive component
  - lines 5–6: page-bound communication

- paragraph 2, line 8:   minimal direct relevance
  - 9: aspiring manager
  - 10: specialist discipline
  - 16: mechanical process

- paragraph 4, lines 5–6: the wheat that has to be . . . separated from the chaff
- paragraph 8, line 2: sift through
- paragraph 9, line 13: take pride of place
               17: deferential response

2. Explain in other words what the following mean:
- paragraph 7, line 7: stretch your legs
               9: thirty-minute stints
- paragraph 9, line 8: 'puff' mail
               22: a 'feel'
               38: 'blurb'

D. Check your grammar

> **Remember**
> He cannot keep in touch without good lines of communication.
> Without good lines of communication, he cannot keep in touch.

Explain the differences of *emphasis* between these two statements. Then form the alternative versions for the following examples and explain them. Is there any difference in *meaning*?
- To the above list, the aspiring manager would probably add a few textbooks.
- Without this awareness, he cannot manage.
- Within the broad purpose of reading for action fall the letters requiring answers.
- For every manager who writes a report, there is a presupposed reader.
- Included in this category are such things as daily carbons.
- Your audience will go to sleep if you speak for too long.
- No one will read your report if the argument is too complicated.
- You should only put up the price if you are sure sales will not fall off.
- Don't do it unless you are quite sure it will work.
- A good manager always informs his staff when he intends to make changes that will affect them.

E. Understanding a lecture

Listen to the lecture on your tape, in which the lecturer introduces the topic of **management**. Then look at the questions below and listen again to the tape, section by section, making notes on the answers. You can listen as many times as you need, and fill out your answers into complete sentences to form a summary of what the lecturer says.

Section 1
- What two reasons does the lecturer think might make you want to become a manager?

Section 2
- How does he propose to deal with the topic of management?

Section 3
- What definition does he offer?
- Does he think this definition is very helpful?

Section 4
- Does a manager's own personality have any influence on the way he manages?

Section 5
- What are the three basic components of scientific management?

Section 6
- Why is scientific knowledge limited?
- Is it useful in running a business?

Section 7
- What term do we now use to describe the uses of science?
- Is this always beneficial?

F. Understanding a printed text (2)

B. WRITING

1 The organization of either a letter or a report requires prior thought. If a letter is a response, then the first step is obviously to refer back to the original, to set the scene. Where the original letter contains a series of questions or statements, a practical way of organizing the response is to follow the same sequence. Sometimes however there is one overwhelmingly important comment to make: this should usually precede the less important detailed points. When you come to the end of what you have to say, stop. Too many otherwise well-written letters or reports are spoilt by the writer's not knowing when to stop.

   A complicated letter—either an initiating one or a response—and all reports, require a more positive approach. In these cases it is always worth taking time to prepare a framework, a skeleton, before starting to write.

   Frameworks can vary from a sequence of self-imposed questions to the more formal 'objectives, facts, opinions, conclusions, and recommendations'. One way or the other, the framework sets out the logic of the material to be written. Without a predetermined framework the writing can be organized and logical, but undoubtedly this is more easily achieved with a framework. Why, therefore, make life more difficult than it need be? Start from a framework. It is always better to know what you are going to write before you put pen to paper. The framework puts you in that position: it is the disciplined arrangement of your thoughts. It is as important as the actual writing—and often perhaps more difficult.

   Knowing what you want to say—and indeed, having something to say—is of course a prerequisite of ordering that material into the framework.

Designing a framework

Defining your reader

2. We have already suggested the simplest framework for a responsive letter. More important are the letters you yourself initiate. One fairly simple framework for an initiating letter, intended to 'sell' something—an idea, a product, or yourself—is the question-and-answer approach. This approach is also suitable for the short report, responding to an instruction to 'Let me have a *short* report on . . .'.

The question-and-answer approach is as simple as it sounds. The first step is to decide what you think the reader will want to know (and once again, this emphasizes the importance of identifying your reader, at least by type). Phrase these requirements as a series of questions, e.g.:

- Why is this letter or report being written?
- What is this idea all about? (Why hasn't it been thought of before?)
- Why should I say yes?
- What's in it for me/us? (That is, what will be the benefits?)
- What other effects will implementation have?
- How long will it take?
- What will it cost? What are other requirements—staff, space, etc?
- What are the consequences of rejecting the idea?

Then rearrange the order of the questions as seems most appropriate to the receiver of the letter or report. As listed above they may or may not be in a suitable order. (Of course, other circumstances may suggest other types of question.)

The next step is to answer the questions. Sometimes it is worth including the questions themselves as subheadings in the text. In other circumstances the replies can be so phrased that the question is implied. Some answers will be simple statements of fact, e.g., the cost. Other questions may require answers that put the case for and against and reach a recommendation. These two kinds of answers—factual and opinion/recommendation—must be clearly identified as such. Never try to pass off opinion as fact, no matter how convinced you are that you are right.

Structuring a report

3. The implied question framework is probably the most suitable for a short (say two-page) often unsolicited report and for most longish letters. It would not be appropriate for a report on a piece of research work, for a project feasibility report or for any such major report. For such reports a more formal framework is required and there are many varieties of these. This is right and proper as the report should fit the need rather than be forced to fit into an inappropriate predetermined framework.

Accepting that each report needs its own unique framework, a general structure might be as follows (see Fig. 2.2):

1. *Introduction*. A statement of what is in the report and perhaps its relationship to other reports.

2. *Terms of reference*. Clear instructions are essential prerequisites of a good report, outlining the objective of the report and the area it is to cover. (If asked to produce a report without terms of reference, it is worth while drafting them briefly yourself and then seeking agreement to them.)

```
       REPORT                              ACTIVITY

   ┌──────────────┐
   │ INTRODUCTION │
   ├──────────────┤
   │  TERMS OF    │ ◄────────────── ┌───────────┐
   │  REFERENCE   │                 │ OBJECTIVE │
   ├──────────────┤                 └─────┬─────┘
   │ BACKGROUND   │ ◄────────────── ┌─────▼─────┐
   │ INFORMATION  │                 │  PROBLEM  │
   ├──────────────┤                 └─────┬─────┘
   │              │                       │
   │              │ ◄────────────── ┌─────▼──────────┐
   │    FACTS     │                 │ INVESTIGATION  │
   │              │                 └─────┬──────────┘
   │              │ ◄────────────── ┌─────▼─────┐
   │              │                 │ ANALYSIS  │
   └──────┬───────┘                 └─────┬─────┘
          │                               │
   ┌──────▼───────┐                 ┌─────▼──────────┐
   │   OPINIONS   │ ◄────────────── │ INTERPRETATION │
   ├──────────────┤                 └────────────────┘
   │ CONCLUSIONS  │
   ├──────────────┤
   │RECOMMENDATIONS│
   └──────────────┘
```

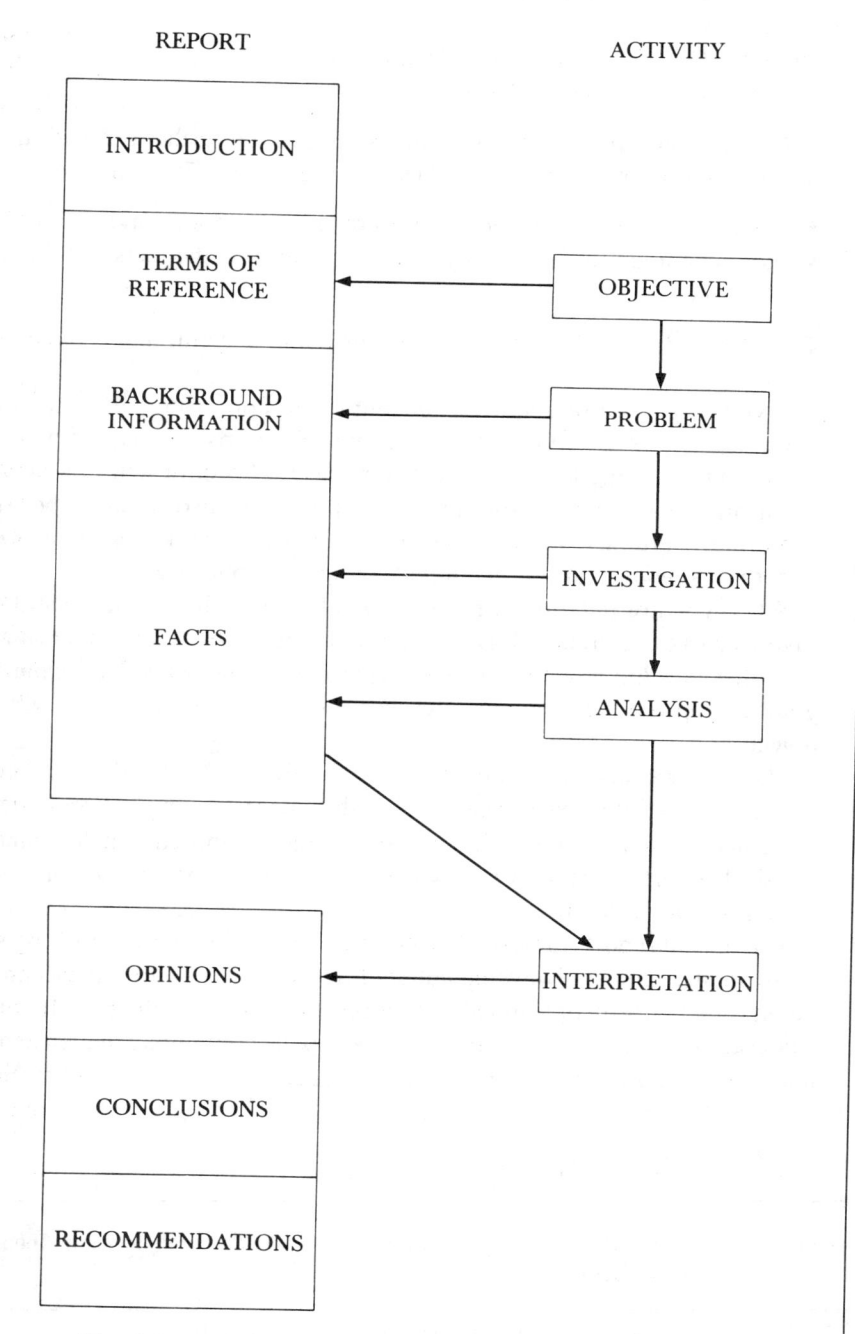

Fig. 2.2 A typical framework for a management report

3. *Background information*. A short history of the subject, a geographical description, the reason why a report is necessary, the problem, etc.
4. *Facts*. Factual results of investigations, observations, tests, etc. Analysis of these facts.
5. *Opinions*. Interpretations of the facts, by the writer; the arguments leading to the:
6. *Conclusions*. In turn, these lead on to:
7. *Recommendations*. What to do.

The opinions, arguments and conclusions may be further debated; the background information and the facts should not be. They must be:

- clearly presented, i.e., not open to misinterpretation; and
- not open to doubt. Procedures used to determine the facts should be described.

There should never be any possibility of opinions being interpreted as facts.

If your organization requires frequent reports on matters of a similar nature, or series of reports (such as progress reports), it may be worth while standardizing the framework for these. Not only will this standardization make comparisons more easy but it may also stimulate better reporting. Certainly, a more appropriate standard framework than the general one above can be developed for specific purposes.

When you are initiating a report yourself, you will obviously not be given terms of reference. It is even more important therefore to be quite sure that you know what you are trying to do, and why. You should yourself replace the terms of reference with a clear definition of your objective.

The longer a report, the more the need to split it up into self-contained sections. Subdivide wherever it helps the understanding process, but remember, subdivisions will not save a badly worded, unclear and illogical report, whereas a well-written, concise report will sometimes manage without them.

The formal report framework itself indicates the initial subdivisions—these should almost always be adhered to. However, within these, the background information and facts sections can often usefully be split up. The mere presence of subheadings breaks up the continuous sequence of paragraphs and increases interest.

G. Check your understanding

Read the passage through carefully, looking up anything you do not understand. Then answer the following questions:

1. Where in a report should the most important point be placed?
2. What often spoils potentially good letters?

3. What is the function of a framework for writing?
4. How important is it to have a framework?
5. What is the first step in designing a question-and-answer approach?
6. Is it important to distinguish between what you *think* and what you *know*?
7. What sort of structure does a research report require?
8. From Figure 2.2, what should a report do with the facts stated?
9. Is it necessary to state how facts have been ascertained?
10. Why should you divide a report into several parts?

H. Understanding discourse

Listen to your tape, on which the Managing Director is describing the company site. Then look at the plan below and label all the buildings etc. that he names. Then look at the questions underneath the plan, go through the tape again making notes for your answers, and finally write them up in complete sentences.

The company site

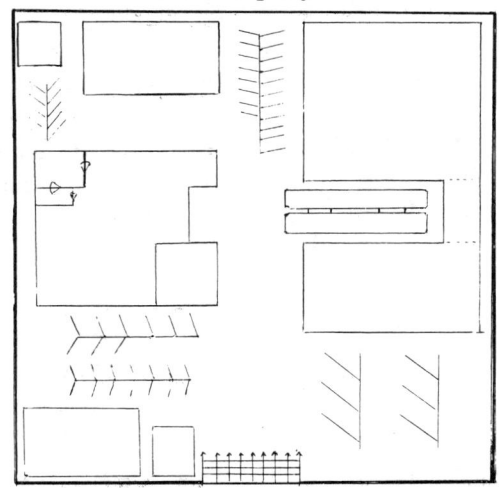

Entrance

1. Why is there such a large gate?
2. What is the large building in the middle on the left?
3. Where is the MD's office?
4. Where is the computer block?
5. Whose offices are between the factory and the warehouse?
6. If you were invited to visit the site, where would you park your car?
7. Where do lorries park?
8. How would you get from the gate to the staff club?
9. If you were in the computer block, how would you get off the site?
10. If you were going to have lunch with the MD, where would you eat?

> This passage in sections A and F of this unit were taken (edited) from WELLS, *How to Communicate*, McGraw-Hill, 1986

UNIT 9
ILLUSTRATING THE POINT

A. Understanding a printed text (1)

The following text returns to the subject of **visual aids**, first touched on in Unit 5. Read quickly through it, paying attention to the way it is constructed and especially to the illustrations and captions. Then answer the following general questions, remembering that you do not have to understand every word of the text in order to do so.

1. What is the purpose of this text?
2. What does Figure 10.1 contain?
3. Which items in Figure 10.2 have previously been introduced in this book?
4. What does Figure 10.3 illustrate?

CLARIFYING THE ISSUE

Describing even a simple object to someone who has never seen it can be extraordinarily difficult. If you try to describe several different objects and their relationship to each other, this becomes even more of a problem. So even when speaking or making a presentation to a small group of people, it is useful to have some sort of drawing or picture to illustrate what you mean. Such drawings etc. are collectively called *visual aids* (or *visuals*, for short). Written business reports and papers make extensive use of such aids, as do advertising and promotion pieces.

Visual aids

1   The form of a drawing for a visual aid can either be one of the varieties of pictorial representation of an actual artefact or natural condition (a map), or it can be one of the diagrammatic presentations of—usually—numerical facts. Falling outside both of these categories are the most wordy, less visual, algorithms and flow-charts.

The forms of pictorial representation in common use are as follows (see Fig. 10.1.):

1. *Orthographic drawings*. These are the plan, side, and end views (drawn strictly to scale) that are familiar to all users of engineering drawings. They are seldom appropriate for management communication.
2. *Perspective drawings*. These drawings represent the object as seen by the normal eye. Just as railway-lines converge into the distance, so too, to a lesser degree, do parallel lines in a perspective drawing. They are less often appropriate for management communication than the simpler isometric drawings.

Fig. 10.1 Types of pictorial representation commonly used in management reports

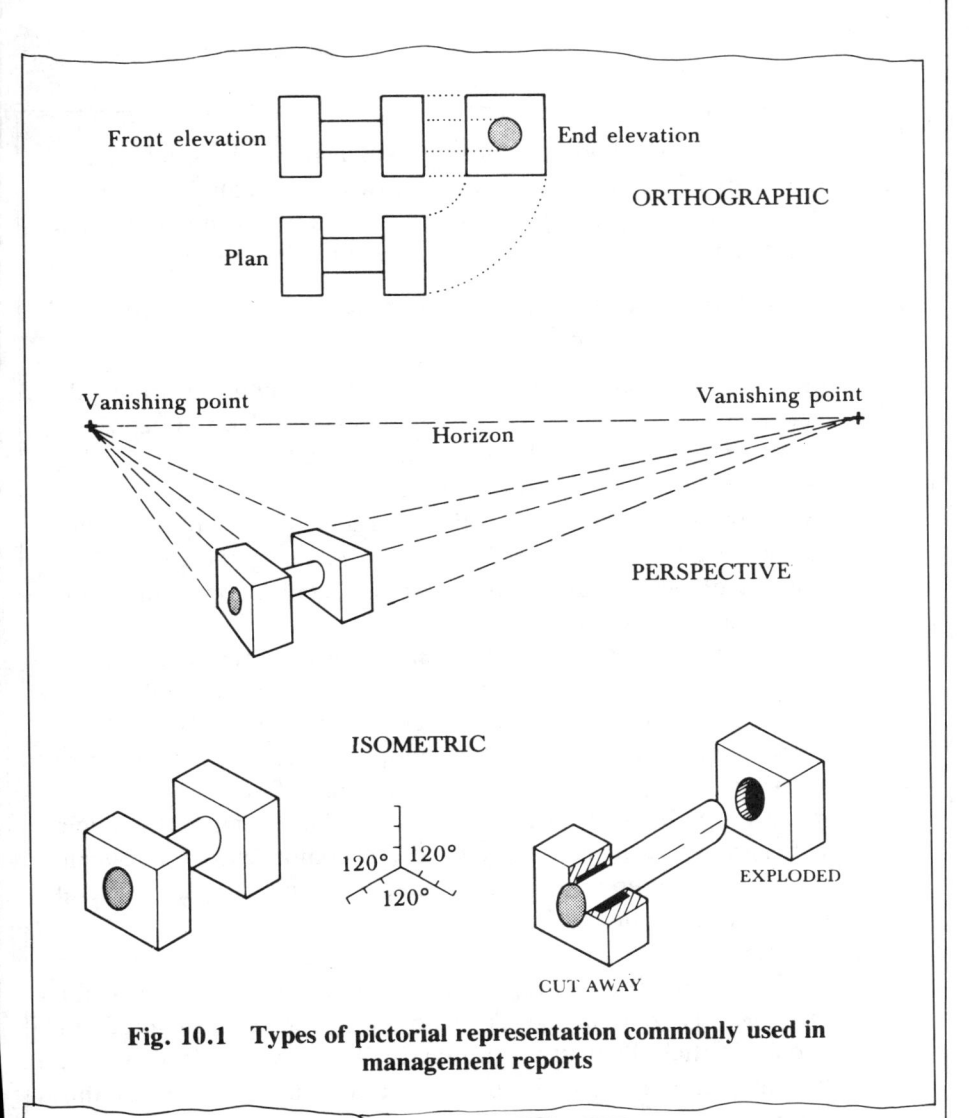

3. *Isometric drawings*. In these, all parallel lines, on whichever face, remain parallel. The three main axes are drawn at 120-degree intervals. For small objects an isometric drawing is almost as effective as a perspective drawing. Often they are most appropriate for management communication—simple to produce, effective, and easy to interpret. (Dimensions can be measured directly from an isometric drawing.)

4. *Exploded and cut-away drawings*. These techniques are usually applied to isometric drawings. Exploded drawings show parts of an artefact before they are assembled, separated, and displayed in order along the appropriate axis. Cut-away drawings are of an assembled artefact but with covers and/or parts of the whole notionally removed to show the interior.

5. *Maps* (including both formalized maps and rough sketch-maps). These are effectively orthographic drawings of natural conditions. As long as they are kept simple and not cluttered up with detail irrelevant to their purpose, maps are admirable illustrations.

2   Diagrammatic presentations of numerical facts commonly used include the following (see Fig. 10.2.):

1. *Graphs*. The best-known and most effective way of illustrating the relationship between two series of numerical facts. Graphs are easily understood and relatively simple to prepare. They are ideal management communication material.
2. *Histograms*. These are a statistically acceptable way of presenting quantities and their relationship to one another by the area and the location of rectangular blocks. (For more details of both graphs and histograms, see **Unit 5**.
3. *Bar charts*. Bar charts are a variation on the histogram and are often more easily understood. They are very good for presenting and comparing quantities visually, but are not normally used for demonstrating the relationship between them. They are best used for demonstrating, e.g., total numbers of vehicles owned in countries A, B, and C in a given year. An elaboration on the simple bar chart divides up each bar into several components. An example might be the composition of an elected body, by parties, in several consecutive elections.
4. *Pictograms*. These are a very visual, but easily misused, way of showing quantities of several items. The ideal pictogram uses, for example, stylized silhouettes of people to represent hundreds of people. Partial silhouettes represent smaller quantities. If, however, the unit picture is varied in size to indicate different quantities, this can very easily be misinterpreted.

5. *Pie charts*. Pie charts are an ideal way of displaying the composition of a whole. If 65, 20, and 15 per cent were the proportions of, perhaps, total sales of a product in its three major markets, they could be presented as segments of a circular 'pie'. (To convert percentages to degrees, simply multiply by 3.6.) An elaboration of the pie chart is, for emphasis, to partially remove one of the 'slices'. Pie charts are sometimes varied in size to represent—in the first example—value of total sales of different products. Here again though, the pictogram-size interpretation problem can arise.

BAR CHARTS

Year 0: 35%
Year 5: 30%
Year 10: 25%

XL Car Co. share of UK market

Bid →
Accepted →
80% grant on expenditure above threshold
Threshold →

Principles of sewage-grant payments to district councils

PICTOGRAM

Year 5
Year 10

Hundreds of staff employed

PIE CHARTS

UK counter sales
UK mail order
Overseas sales

Total sales Year 3

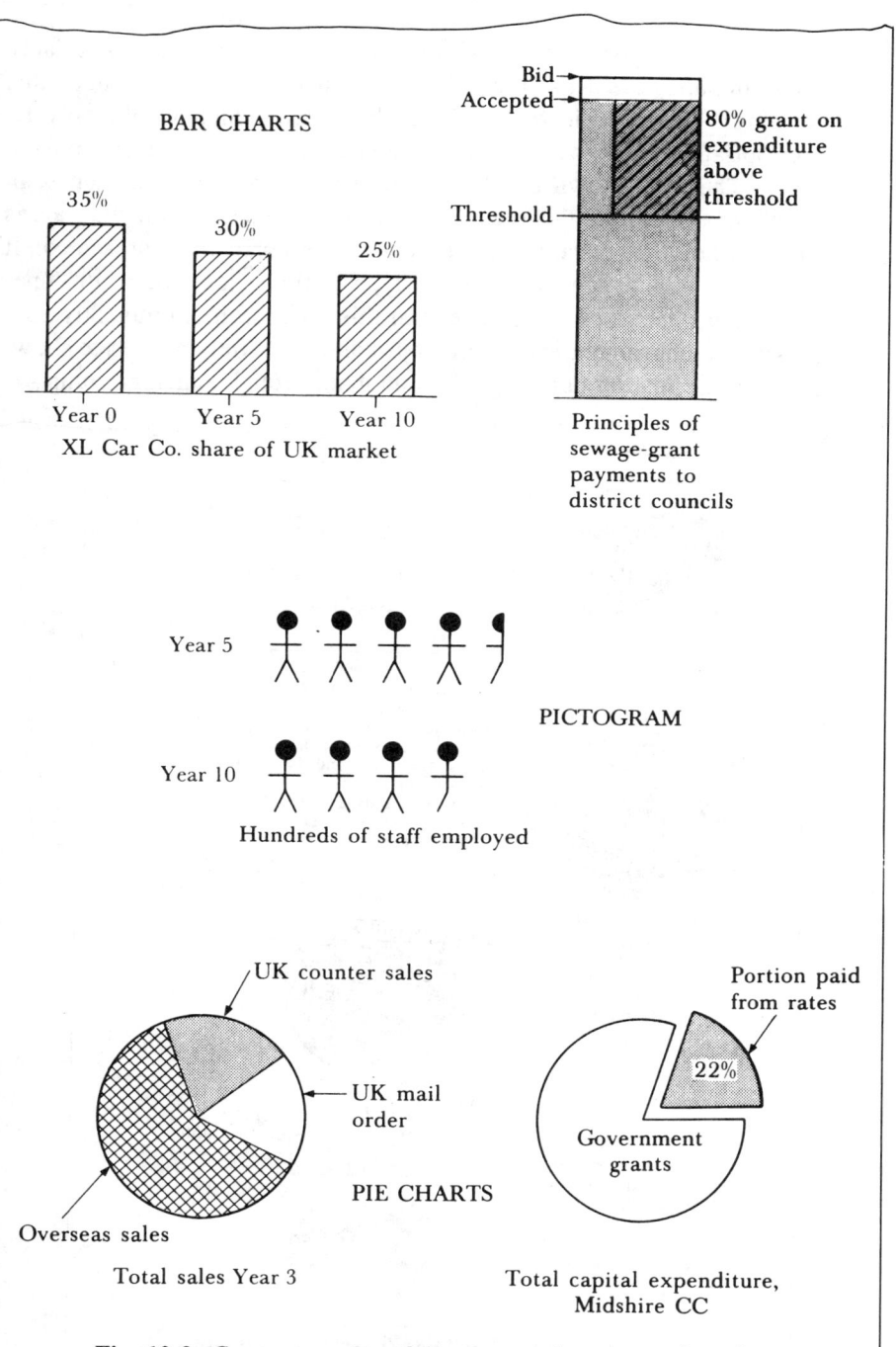

Portion paid from rates
22%
Government grants

Total capital expenditure, Midshire CC

Fig. 10.2 Some examples of diagrammatic presentation of numerical facts

3   Not always a presentation of numerical information but invariably diagrammatic, are what are sometime called schematics. Under this heading would be electrical-wiring diagrams, which would only be appropriate in very specialized management reports, and diagrammatic maps. The well-known London Underground diagrammatic map is an excellent example of this type. There is no pretence that the diagram is to scale nor that distances or directions are correctly represented. It exists to show which lines serve which stations, and where the line-interchange facilities are situated. In this purpose it is eminently successful. A diagrammatic map might just as successfully be used to show, for instance, the production path of an item through a factory complex.

Stores control flowchart

Fig. 10.3 Stores control flowchart

RECEPTION BAY

Central point where goods/materials are housed, to be released to the works against stores requisitions and issued accompanied by stores issue notes. The receipt and issue of goods/materials are logged on stores records, so that their balances can be easily ascertained.

Materials received and recorded

STORES DEPARTMENT

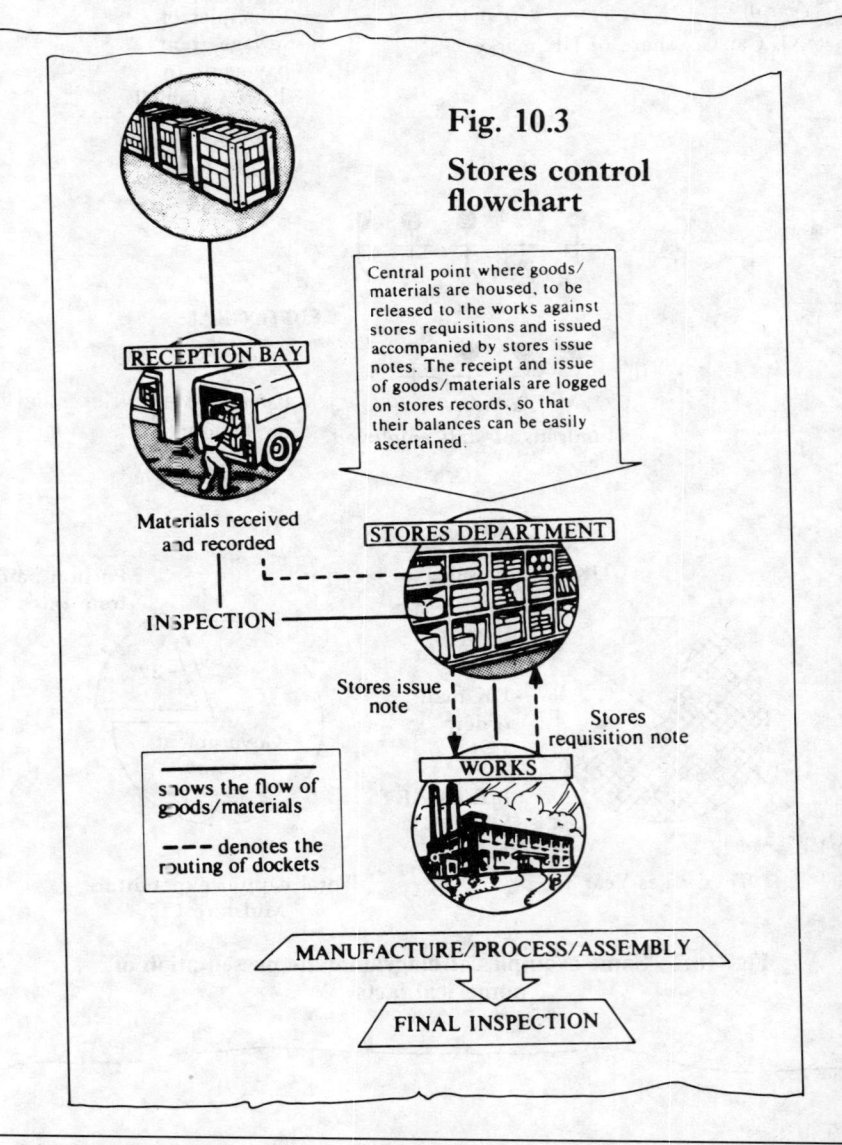

INSPECTION

Stores issue note

Stores requisition note

WORKS

— shows the flow of goods/materials
--- denotes the routing of dockets

MANUFACTURE/PROCESS/ASSEMBLY

FINAL INSPECTION

Taken from TROTMAN, Modern Secretarial Procedures, McGraw-Hill, 1986

B. Check your understanding

Re-read the passage carefully, looking up anything you do not understand. Then answer the following questions.

1. What is the purpose of using a visual aid?
2. Are orthographic drawings very useful to business managers?
3. What does a perspective drawing show?
4. What is an exploded drawing?
5. What is a cutaway drawing?
6. What should be avoided if a map is to be useful?
7. What makes graphs ideal material for management communications?
8. Are histograms statistically acceptable?
9. What is the main use of bar charts?
10. Give an example of a suitable use of a bar chart.
11. In what way may a pictogram be misleading?
12. What is the ideal use of a pie chart?
13. How do you convert percentages to degrees?
14. Look at Figure 10.2 and say:
    - What happened to the XL Car Co share of the UK market between years 5 and 10?
    - Roughly how many fewer staff were employed, according to the pictogram, in year 10 as opposed to year 5?
    - What proportion of Midshire County Council expenses were paid by government grants?
15. Look at Figure 10.3 and say:
    - Where do materials go between the reception bay and the stores?
    - What does the figure tell you about the relative distances between the reception bay, the stores department and the works?

C. Increase your vocabulary

Explain in your own words what the following mean as used in the text. You will need to look some of them up in a dictionary:

- paragraph 1, line 2: pictorial representation
                   artefact
               3: diagrammatic presentations
               4: numerical facts
               5: algorithms

- paragraph 1.1, line 1: orthographic
                     2: drawn strictly to scale

- paragraph 1.2, line 5: isometric

- Figure 10.1: front/end elevation

- paragraph 1.3, lines 2–3: drawn at 120-degree intervals

- paragraph 1.4, line 6: notionally removed

- paragraph 1.5, line 1: formalized maps

- paragraph 2.4, line 3: stylized silhouettes

- paragraph 3, line 2: schematics
             11: production path

D. Check your grammar

Remember the 'degrees'

Positive	Comparative	Superlative
little	less	least
some/—	more	most
good/well	better	best
small	smaller	smallest

Now list the other degrees in the following table:

Positive	Comparative	Superlative
		most wordy
	less visual	
	to a lesser degree	
	less often	
		most appropriate
		best known
		most effective
		best used
	better value	

E. Understanding a lecture

Play through the lecture on your tape. It is split into a number of sections to make it easier to use. Then look at the questions below and play the tape again, section by section, noting down answers to the questions. You can fill up your notes later to form complete sentences as a summary of the most important points.

Section 1
- What does 'behavioural' mean?

Section 2
- What two things does the lecturer say that a business does?
- What is a 'service' business?

Section 3
- What is meant by 'job satisfaction'?
- Why do people work?

Section 4
- What is behavioural management based on?
- What use can a manager make of the findings of psychologists and sociologists?

Section 5
- How should a manager treat his staff?
- What natural ability should a good manager have?

Section 6
- Is the concept of behavioural management a useful one?

F. Understanding a printed text (2)

MORE VISUAL AIDS

1 Most of the visuals we have seen so far are suitable especially for inclusion in reports and papers, but there are other, larger-scale aids of a more permanent nature. A good example is the use of a charting board.

Most charting boards help their users to exert control over situations and operations by visual summaries of past, present and planned future developments. Thus displays are designed to enable managers to see quickly the current state of affairs, to be able to seize on points where delays in assignments are building up, and to diagnose difficulties so that they can give immediate instructions for action to remedy them. Types of situations where constant checking and control are necessary include: stock and supply keeping; financial expenditure over a set period; maintaining and servicing plant, equipment or vehicles; machine loading (i.e., the amount of work, estimated in hours or days, allocated to computers or other machines in office, factory or workshop); location of staff; production of goods; or any other project where timing is important.

Even where a static situation is portrayed—e.g., in a staff holiday rota—a chart can be much more helpful than a list. For example, the number of staff to be away at any one time will be obvious; adequate cover of duties can be assured if distinctive signals are used for different categories of staff; additional leave can be fitted into periods easily seen to be not yet taken up; the reasons for anticipated absences can be shown by using different symbols for holidays, business trips, training courses, etc.

Purpose

Axes

2 Since the time element is so important, most control boards have a time axis; this usually runs from left to right across the top of the chart. As in Figure 20.9 the board is divided into vertical sections or columns for the units of time involved, which may be months, weeks or days—or occasionally years or hours, according to the type of situation or job charted. The top axis might, of course, indicate other measurements instead—e.g., quantities in stock control charts. The horizontal divisions or channels may represent the parts of the job to be completed, the different machines or personnel concerned in it, or various items of plant or stock to be repaired, serviced or stored.

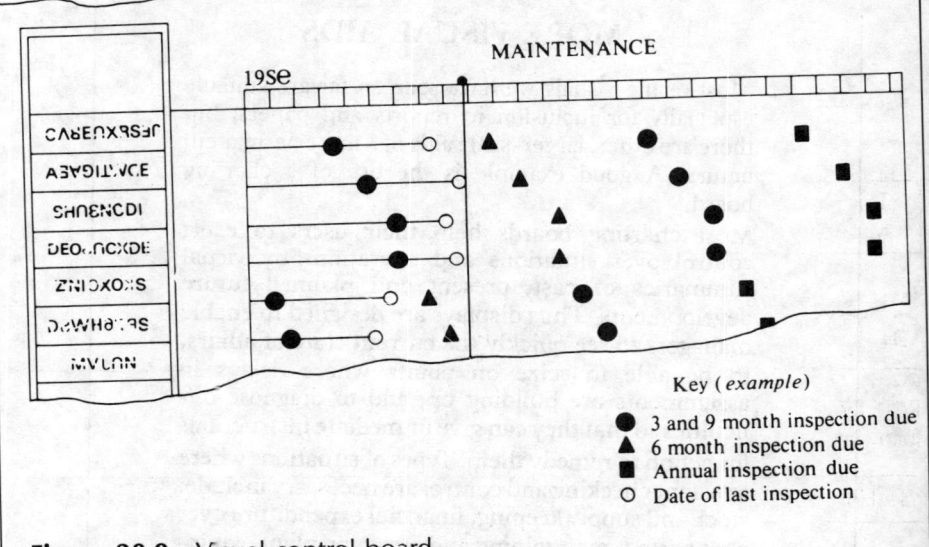

Figure 20.9 Visual control board.

Key (*example*)
- ● 3 and 9 month inspection due
- ▲ 6 month inspection due
- ■ Annual inspection due
- ○ Date of last inspection

Signals

3 These are the symbols used on the chart. They are fixed to the visual display board, in appropriate positions. Signals can be of many shapes, materials and colours. The signals in Figure 20.9 are circular, square, or triangular, and appear either to be plugged into the board or fixed to it magnetically. Actual words or numbers can be written or typed on pieces of card. Some of these have a plastic top bar enabling them to be fitted into a wire grid across the board's surface. Others are T-shaped and inserted into slots, only the crossbar bearing the essential

details remaining visible. Colour coding may be used to indicate types of information.
Laminated board surfaces allow written characters to be easily deleted and substituted. Another method uses small discs or wheels, bearing numbers on their narrow edges, which can be rotated to show the desired figures.

4 Unless signals actually bear information in the form of letters, words or numbers, a key to their significance must be provided, as the information they denote differs according to the users' needs. Even the use of markers or pins on a wall map indicating the location of a firm's branches, agents, or representatives needs to be explained.

Keys

This passage was taken (edited) from TROTMAN, *Modern Secretarial Procedures*, McGraw-Hill, 1986

G. Check your understanding

Read the text carefully, looking up anything you do not understand. Then answer the following questions:

1. How do charting boards help in controlling operations?
2. What do they help one to see at a glance?
3. Why is constant control of stock essential?
4. Can a charting board be used to show where members of staff are?
5. Why are different symbols used?
6. How is the time factor usually shown?
7. What do the solid circles in Figure 20.9 show?
8. What do the squares indicate?
9. What is the purpose of the key?
10. What do you understand by 'colour coding'?

H. Understanding discourse

Listen to the talk on your tape, which explains the working of a mailing room, and follow what the speaker says by looking at the drawing in your book. Then answer the questions underneath the drawing:

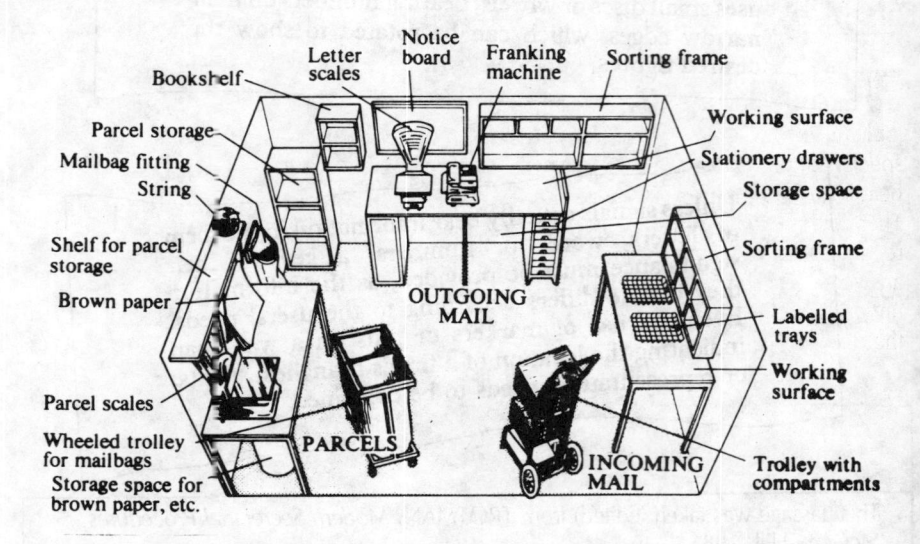

Labels on drawing: Bookshelf, Letter scales, Notice board, Franking machine, Sorting frame, Working surface, Parcel storage, Stationery drawers, Mailbag fitting, Storage space, String, Shelf for parcel storage, Sorting frame, Brown paper, OUTGOING MAIL, Labelled trays, Working surface, Parcel scales, Wheeled trolley for mailbags, PARCELS, INCOMING MAIL, Trolley with compartments, Storage space for brown paper, etc.

Drawing from TROTMAN, *Modern Secretarial Procedures*, McGraw-Hill, 1986

1.
   - Why is efficient handling of the mail important to a business?
   - What was the original meaning of 'post'?
   - What is the difference between 'post' and 'mail'?
   - What dictates the layout of a post room?
   - What should staff *not* have to do?
   - Is a post room equally busy all day?
   - When is the mail usually delivered?
   - When does the collection of the mail usually take place?
   - What is meant by 'internal mail'?
   - Has the use of mechanised handling of the mail eliminated all errors?

2. Look up the following expressions and write short definitions:
   - mailing plan
   - mailing list
   - mailing shot
   - direct mail

Passage A was taken (edited) from WELLS, *Learning to Communicate*, McGraw-Hill, 1986

CATCHING THE EYE

UNIT 10

A. Understanding a printed text (1)

Look at the following text, which concerns **publicity matter**, paying attention to the way it is divided into parts and to the illustrations, captions and headings. Then answer the following general questions about it, remembering that you do not have to have understood every word in order to do so.

1. What is the passage teaching you to do?
2. How does it try to capture a reader's attention?
3. What two kinds of promotion material does it deal with?

INFLUENCING THE READER

Though the basic purpose of a piece of writing may be to *inform* the reader, it may also have another, even a more important aim—to *influence* him, perhaps to take a certain course of action—most commonly, to *buy something*.

To do this, it must first of all attract his attention, and this it will do to a large extent through its own appearance, that is, through its *visual impact*.

Making an Impact

1   The impact of a report will be enhanced not merely be the inclusion of well-located illustrations, but also by the overall layout of the document. Too often, reports are presented as crowded pages of text with an occasional illustration to lighten the strain.

the importance of layout

It is NOT necessary for typed or printed text to extend the full width of a page; margins do NOT have to be small, uniform on each side, or even consistent throughout a document; illustrations do NOT have to be central in the width of a page; and most important of all, well-placed blank space is NEVER a waste. A rule of thumb can be postulated:

25 per cent (more) blank space means 100 per cent more impact

(The figures may be debatable but the principle is indisputable.)

The advantages of blank space are as relevant to pages of words alone as they are to pages with both illustrations and text. A page of words laid out with a very large margin on one side and a small one on the other is not only more attractive than the traditional (and mean-looking) narrow, near-equal margins, but it also provides more space for notes. And we

using blank space

have already recognized that a prudent manager-reader always annotates his papers; by giving the manager some blank space for the notes, our presentation is both helpful and more attractive (see Fig. 10.3).

Designing a Brochure

In reports, and more importantly in brochures, it is always preferable to balance the blocks of text and the illustrations on any one- or two-page spread. A—particularly black-and-white—photograph can sometimes

A (Left) A conventional, dull-looking, solid block of text.

B (Right) Much better: again, only text, but plenty of blank space—between paragraphs, in margin, around lists. It looks 'light' and easy to read.

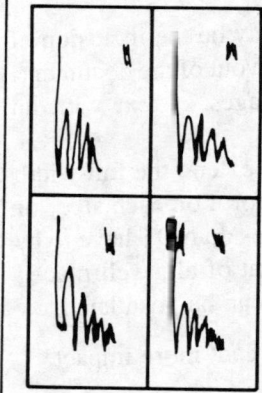

C (Left) An unimaginative two-page spread. The text on the right at least uses some blank space but the illustrations are displayed in a very dull fashion.

appear 'solid' and therefore of heavier 'weight' than the overall greyness of a block of text; a small darker photograph can therefore be balanced by a larger block of grey text. Variety in the sizes of illustrations and blocks of text is always beneficial; consistency in illustration size can well be boring.

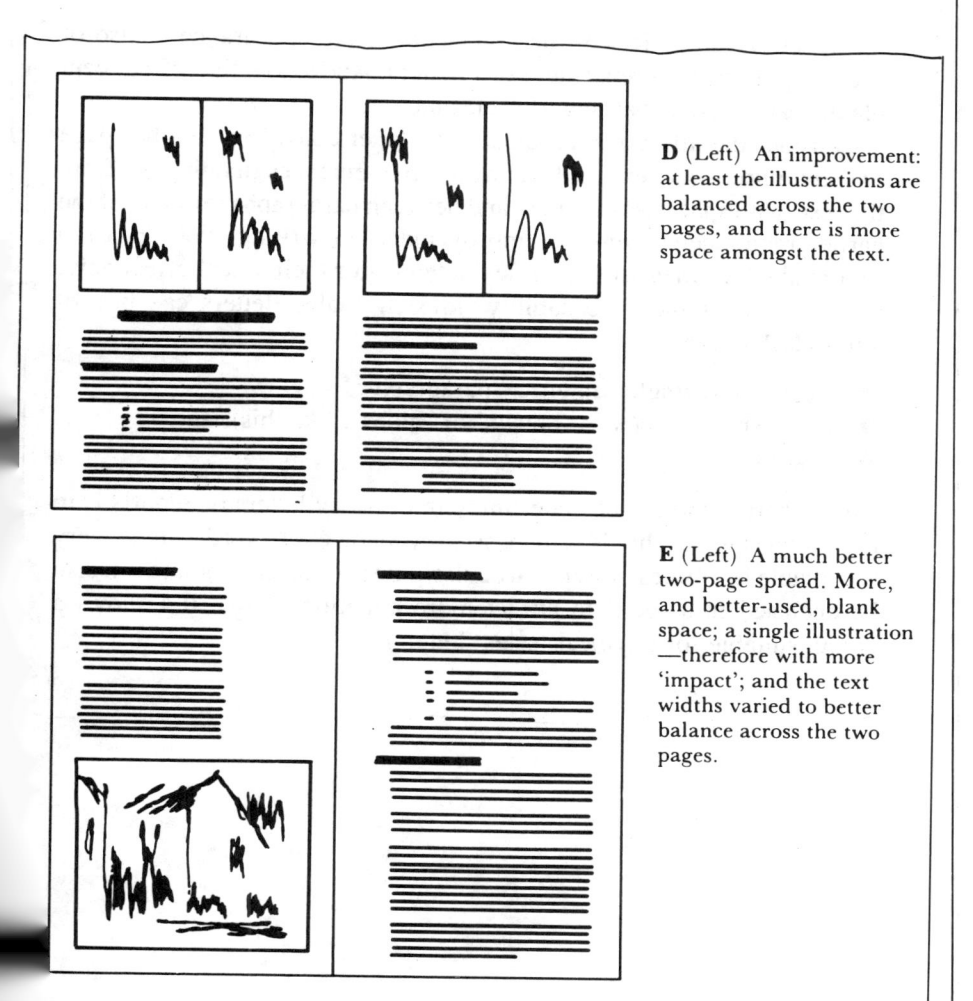

D (Left) An improvement: at least the illustrations are balanced across the two pages, and there is more space amongst the text.

E (Left) A much better two-page spread. More, and better-used, blank space; a single illustration —therefore with more 'impact'; and the text widths varied to better balance across the two pages.

Fig. 10.3 Some examples of page layouts for text alone and for text with illustrations

Designing a Sales Letter

2   Layout and the effect of the immediate visual appearance is also of great importance in preparing 'sales' letters. And again, the '25 per cent blank space' rule is particularly relevant.

Consider the difference in impact of a letter consisting of a full page of solid, unrelieved text, and one with some sentences standing out from the rest, with space around them and between paragraphs. Several of the earlier recommendations for improvements in writing style are even more valuable when writing 'sales' letters—for their visual effect now, as much as for their 'readability' impact. 'Sales' letters can benefit particularly from:

- short—even single-sentence—paragraphs;
- use of short lists (with 'bullets' or 'blobs', like this); and
- headings.

And, whereas the use of underlining in ordinary letters or reports is to be avoided—you should emphasize by choice of words—it is very acceptable in a 'sales' letter. Particularly important sales points can also be enclosed in a 'box' to attract more attention. (Fig. 10.4 shows a layout suitable for a typical 'sales' letter.)

The material in this unit was taken (edited) from WELLS, *How to Communicate*, McGraw-Hill, 1978

BLOGGS and Scribe Ltd

23 Bloggs Street
Mudworth
Mudshire MU1 3QA

Mudworth (0337) 589561

Manufacturers of Quality Office Equipment since 1940

** FREE 'VOICETYPER' TRIAL **

AND

REPLY WITHIN FOURTEEN DAYS FOR

** FREE MYSTERY GIFT **

Dear Reader

What have you got to lose? We know that the new BLOGGS & SCRIBE 'Voicetyper' will change your life. To prove it ... we are offering you the chance of a month's free trial.

If, unbelievably, you are not 'hooked' on this 'Tomorrow's Typewriter Today' - just send it back, at our expense, within four weeks. But we know you will want to keep it ...

What will it do?

The BLOGGS & SCRIBE 'Voicetyper' does what its name implies:

> It types from the sound of your voice!

No other machine in the world will produce perfect typescript - just like this letter, which was produced by the Voicetyper - from your voice alone!

> The world's greatest inventors have strived for years to produce a writing machine that does not require human intervention between thoughts and paper. Now, at last, they have succeeded. The BLOGGS & SCRIBE 'Voicetyper' is the result - and it is available to you!
>
> NOW!

How do I get one?

All you have to do to get your own 'Voicetyper' - on totally risk-free trial - is fill in the enclosed form and send it to us, BLOGGS & SCRIBE, in the reply paid envelope.

Send no money now ... we will debit your bank account - direct - after the free month's trial. AND ... if you reply NOW, within fourteen days ... we will send you ...

Fig. 10.4 Typical layout—and content—of a 'sales' letter, using short paragraphs and 'boxed' comments

B. Check your understanding

Read through the text carefully, looking up anything you do not understand. Then answer the questions given below.

1. Introductory passage and paragraph 1:
   - What two purposes may a piece of writing have?
   - What must it first do if it wishes to influence the reader?
   - What do you understand by 'visual impact'?
   - How can the visual impact of a report be enhanced?
   - Should typed pages always be filled up?
   - Must the margins be even and consistent throughout?
   - Should you put the illustrations always in the middle of a page?
   - Is blank space a waste of paper?
   - What practical use can be made of a wide margin?
   - What would be a good way to balance a very dark photograph?
   - Does keeping all the illustrations the same size make a page look interesting?

2. Look at the sample page layouts:
   - Why is B better than A?
   - Why does the author consider C to be dull?
   - In what way is D an improvement over C?
   - What makes the author think that E is the best?
   - Do you agree?

3. Paragraph 2:
   - What is the '25 per cent blank space' rule?
   - What sort of sentences are recommended for sales letters?
   - Why?
   - How are main points emphasised in the ordinary letters?
   - And in a sales letter?
   - What are boxes used for in sales letters?

4. Look at the sample sales letter:
   - Pick out the words underlined. What do they show?
   - Why is the statement in the middle of the letter placed in a box?
   - Is the letter easy to read?
   - Does it make you interested in what it is selling?
   - Have you spotted the grammatical error?

C. Increase your vocabulary

Explain in your own words the meaning of the following, as used in the text:

- paragraph 1, line 2: well-located illustrations
                        overall layout
             9: rule of thumb
                        postulated
             11: debatable
                        indisputable
             17: prudent manager-reader

- Figure 10.3A: conventional

- paragraph 2, line 5: unrelieved text
             9: 'readability' impact

D. Check your grammar

> **Remember**
> We shall need *some* extra staff for this project.
> We shall *not* need *any* extra staff for this project.

Make alternative forms for the following, using *some* or *any* correctly and making the necessary changes in the rest of the sentence to show that you understand the construction. You will be helped in the first few examples:

- You should { always include { some illustrations in your reports.
               { never   { any
- A report { without any illustrations is { always dull.
           { with some   { never
- { Fortunately, I had some pictures to show the audience.
  { Unfortunately,
- The graph did not seem to show any significant changes.
- Our chairman rarely has anything interesting to say.
- It is helpful if there are some blank spaces for notes.
- A leaflet is likely to have some visual impact if it is well laid out.
- It will not generate any sales if no one reads it.

E. Understanding a lecture

Listen to the lecture on your tape. It is divided into several sections to make it easier to understand. You may play it through section by section. Then say:

1. What definitions of a system does the lecturer give?
2. What nine kinds of management skills does he quote?

F. Understanding a printed text (2)

English For Academic Purposes Series

The *English for Academic Purposes Series* aims to prepare students in tertiary education, at an intermediate level of English, to undertake a course in a special subject in English.

The texts provide enough material for approximately 150 lessons and are divided into 15 units with a Progress Test at the end of units 5 and 10.

All units have reading passages which are all taken from textbooks used at university level. They also contain listening sections and a grammar section which concentrates on structures commonly used in "scientific" English.

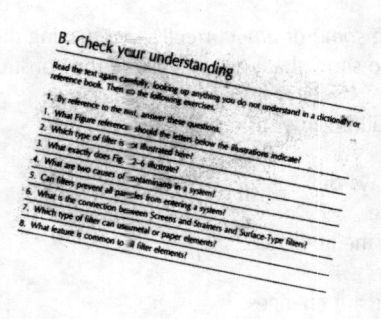

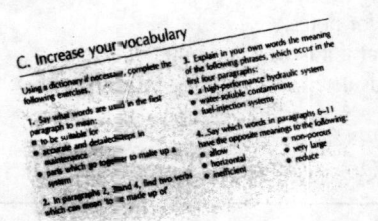

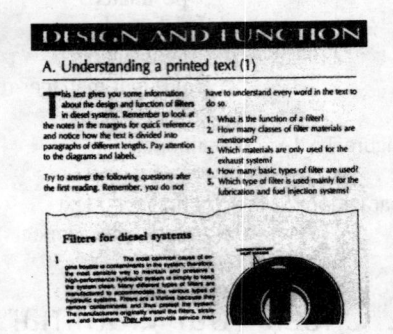

Each unit contains:

A. Understanding a printed Text: gist reading and reading for detailed understanding from authentic source material.

B. Check your Understanding: comprehension exercises.

C. Increase your Vocabulary: a variety of exercises e.g. synonyms; antonyms; explaining terms; etc.

D. Check your Grammar: key structures and tenses; sentence and paragraph writing.

E. Understanding a Lecture; each listening section covers: comprehension; note taking; information transfer exercises; annotation of diagrams and related study skills.

F. Understanding a printed Text (2): continues the topic of the unit and concentrates on detailed understanding.

G. Check your Understanding: a variety of exercises to reinforce comprehension of the subject matter.

H. Understanding Discourse: gives practice in listening to instructions and specific directions.

The Key to Academic Success

The *Series* aims to prepare students for university level courses taught in English. It familiarises students with the kind of texts that are studied at this level and prepares them for the specialist language and vocabulary necessary for understanding texts. The relevant study skills of note taking, summarising, writing up experiments, reports and listening to lectures are all practised in the *English for Academic Purposes Series*.

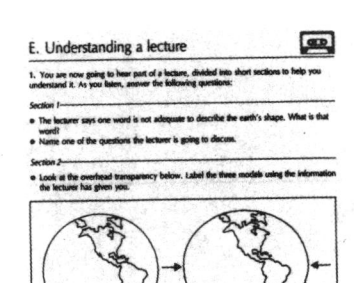

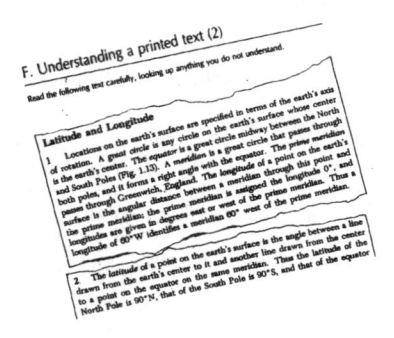

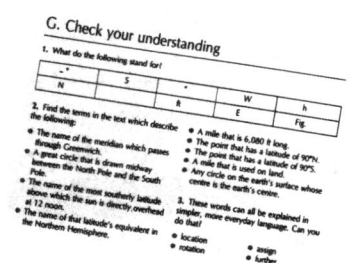

Extracts A, B, C, D taken from General Engineering

Extracts E, F, G, H taken from Earth Sciences

Leaflet material reproduced by courtesy of Cassell Ltd.

G. Check your understanding

Look carefully at the double-page spread from a sales leaflet given in section F. Then answer the questions below (you may find it useful to refer back to sections A and B). Explain your answers.

1. Do the two pages together have a positive visual impact?
2. Is the left-hand page balanced?
3. Is the right-hand page balanced?
4. Is the double-page spread balanced?
5. Are the pages too full?
6. Are the illustrations all the same size?
7. How would you rate the 'readability' of the pages?
8. Why are the book extracts set at angles?
9. Do you think the leaflet is successful?
10. Write a short description of the leaflet as an example of layout.

H. Understanding discourse

Listen to the tutor on your tape talking about leadership. You may play it back as many times as necessary. Then:

1
- List the three types of authority that the tutor quotes.
- Write in the two lots of circles below what he says are the needs and tasks of a leader.

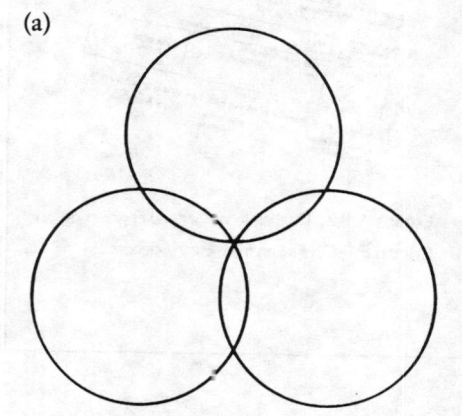

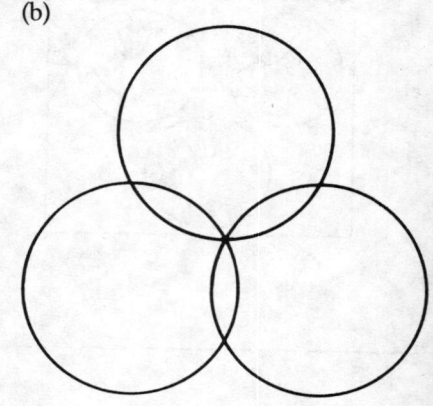

(a)   (b)

Discourse material taken from PRABHU & BAKER, *Improving Business Performance*, McGraw-Hill, 1986

CHECK YOUR PROGRESS 2

The following sections are designed to help you assess your progress. They are not tests that you pass or fail, but they will give you an idea of how you are developing the skills you will need.

A. Reading

Read the following passage, then answer the questions, showing whether you think the statements are right or wrong, and making your choice from alternative answers.

HOLDING MEETINGS

Much of any manager's time is taken up with meetings. There are meetings with colleagues to agree a course of action. There are meetings with superiors to report and to discuss future policies. There are meetings with subordinates. Many would say that there are far too many meetings: some would be even less polite. There can, however, be no doubt that 5
meetings are part of every manager's life. He should therefore know how to cope with them. He should know the techniques of communication in meetings. He should know how to use these techniques to his own advantage.

It is sometimes suggested that when a manager can't think what to do, 10
he holds a meeting. But meetings in themselves are not an end product, no matter what some may think. They are merely one of many means of management communication. It may well be that a problem can be solved by a one-to-one discussion, face to face, or even by telephone. If the need can be met without a meeting, so be it. 15

Let us therefore define a meeting, in the management sense, as the gathering together of a group of people for a controlled discussion, with a specific purpose. Each of those attending the meeting has a need to be there and both discussion and its result could not be so well achieved in any other way. It is often salutary to calculate the cost of a meeting. A 20
simple meeting of a few people on middle-executive salaries can soon run into three-figure costs for wages alone. Do not, therefore, have unnecessary people sitting in at meetings and do ensure that all meetings are both efficient and effective.

The essentials of effective and efficient meetings are as follows: 25

1. A purpose: there are two basic purposes for all meetings—problem-solving or idea-generating. Both of these can, however, be further subdivided.
2. An agenda: without this essential piece of paper (or list on a blackboard) any meeting will quickly become out of control, and an 30
uncontrolled meeting is most unlikely to be effective or efficient.

3. Members: these essential ingredients can be categorized in three types:

   - the chairman;
   - the secretary; and
   - the other members.

   The people in each of these three categories have their own functions and duties; sometimes they conflict, but no one can operate alone. The members—in all three categories—will be expected to prepare for the meeting and once there, to concentrate, to communicate, and to co-operate, in order that the meeting will generate the next essential . . .
4. A result: the whole object of the exercise, but which will itself be inadequate until it is recorded in the final essential . . .
5. A report: usually those much-maligned minutes.

1. Put a tick or a cross in the box after each statement to show whether you think it is correct or not:
1 Managers are not very often required to attend meetings. ☐
2 Some people think that holding a meeting is an end in itself. ☐
3 It is better to hold a meeting than to try to settle a problem by telephone. ☐
4 A meeting is intended to be a controlled discussion with a definite purpose. ☐
5 The cost of a meeting is not important. ☐
6 Meetings are called either to solve problems or to generate ideas. ☐
7 The purpose of an agenda is to keep a meeting under control. ☐
8 There is never any conflict between members of a committee. ☐
9 Chairman, secretary and members must all co-operate if a meeting is to achieve anything. ☐
10 The end product of a meeting is a written report. ☐

2. Choose the correct definition of the following words as they are used in the text:

1 line 3   a *superior* is someone who is:
   better ☐
   older ☐
   in a higher position ☐
   more intelligent ☐

2 line 4   a *subordinate* is someone who is:
   inferior ☐
   younger ☐
   less intelligent ☐
   in a lower position ☐

3 line 20   *salutary* means: wise ☐
   helpful ☐
   healthy ☐
   polite ☐

4 line 44 *inadequate* means:
                insufficient ☐
                incomplete ☐
                pointless ☐
                inefficient ☐

5 line 45 *maligned* means:
                neglected ☐
                disliked ☐
                unwanted ☐
                spoken badly of ☐

B. Writing

Read the following text, then complete the activities listed below.

The purpose

We have said that there are two basic purposes for meetings—problem-solving and idea-generating. The problem-oriented purpose covers a variety of meetings: the problem may be as simple as how best to explain an already agreed course of action to a group of executives. A face-to-face meeting with all of them at the same time is probably the best solution. The problem-solving meeting may also be to enable the manager to consider a variety of facts or expert opinions and weigh one against the other before making a decision. The only factor common to all so-called problem-oriented meetings is the expectation of some action or decision as a result of it.

The other basic purpose of a meeting is idea-generating. Much more a discussion between equals, there is not necessarily anything concrete to show after such a meeting. The end result is likely to be more a collective wisdom, ideally not over-dominated by the views of any one individual. The actual clash of ideas, the confrontations of subconscious prejudices, will help to generate new and hopefully better thinking.

1. Now look at the visuals (a), (b). (c) and (d), where the arrows indicate the direction of information flow. Write a short statement in your own words of what is going on in each case.

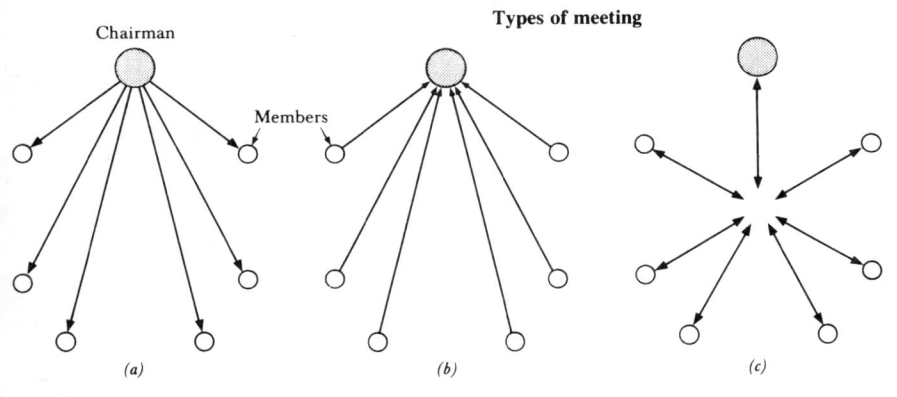

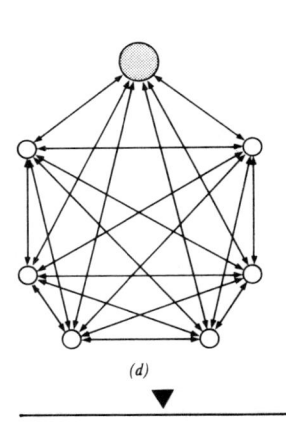

Types of meeting

(a) (b) (c) (d)

2. One of the types of meeting is concerned with generating ideas: the other three are problem-solving meetings. Can you say which is the odd man out?
(a) ☐   (b) ☐   (c) ☐   (d) ☐

3. Say which type of meeting is concerned with: telling ☐
(write a, b, c or d in the boxes)   collecting information ☐
                                                 reaching a concensus ☐
                                                 'brainstorming' ☐

C. Listening

Listen to the lecture on your tape. Then:

1. Say whether the following statements are correct or not by putting a tick or a cross in the boxes:
1 The outcome of a meeting does not depend on the chairman. ☐
2 A democratic chairman is willing to listen to other people. ☐
3 An autocratic chairman does not welcome discussion. ☐
4 A chance for members to express their opinions is given in a concensus seeking meeting. ☐
5 Creative tension is never very productive. ☐
6 A good chairman talks a lot during meetings. ☐
7 An autocratic chairman will not act on decisions he dislikes. ☐
8 In a 'brainstorming', the chairman can talk as much as he wants. ☐
9 Summarising the results of a 'brainstorming' is sometimes impossible. ☐
10 After a 'brainstorming', everyone feels pleased, except the chairman. ☐

2. Choose the correct definitions:
1 an *autocrat* is someone who: always listens to other people ☐
                                      consults his colleagues a lot ☐
                                      always wants his own way ☐
                                      hates making decisions ☐

2 a *concensus* is: a decision that everyone accepts ☐
                           a generally agreed opinion ☐
                           a compromise solution ☐
                           a wise decision ☐

3 *creative tension* is: an argument with the chairman ☐
                                a fight during a committee meeting ☐
                                a disagreement that throws up ideas ☐
                                an exchange of interesting insults ☐

The possible score is 33.
How did you get on? ☐

IT PAYS TO ADVERTISE

UNIT 11

A. Understanding a printed text (1)

In this unit we follow some of the points raised in Unit 5 about the question of **advertising**. Look at the structure of the text, then read quickly through it and note down the answers to the following questions. Remember that you will not need to understand every word in the text in order to do so:

1. Does the author agree with the slogan in the title?
2. Into what larger concept does advertising fit?
3. What is a branded product?

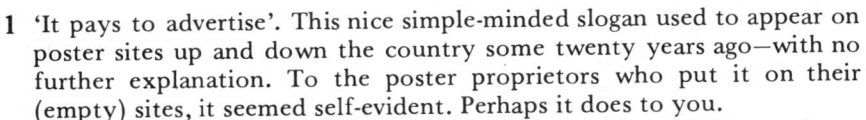

1   'It pays to advertise'. This nice simple-minded slogan used to appear on poster sites up and down the country some twenty years ago—with no further explanation. To the poster proprietors who put it on their (empty) sites, it seemed self-evident. Perhaps it does to you.

   If you are running a business, it may not be so simple. There are plenty of businesses, in all sectors of the economy, which advertise either very little or, indeed, not at all. You do not see many advertisements for Marks & Spencer, and even fewer for British Home Stores—though, of course, their shop windows are their own ads. The fact is that advertisements are just one of the many tools available to help a firm to sell what it has to offer, and it may well be that advertising is, quite simply, not appropriate for the firm's particular circumstances.

Does it?

   At its simplest, a business buys resources, which can be raw materials, parts and components, the brains and muscles of its employees, or even money, turns them into some form of product or service, and sells them to its customers at a profit. To do this, it requires working capital, employees, premises, potential customers, and a means of reaching them. This applies pretty well to any kind of business. The process of identifying, reaching, and selling to the potential customers is, nowadays, called marketing, which is rather more than just the jumped-up name for 'selling' that it is sometimes thought to be.

How business works

   People involved in marketing, who for some reason are often rather defensive about it, spend a great deal of time trying to invent better definitions of their task, in order to make clear to everyone else what it is all about. This is not a very helpful process, as the definitions tend to be ingenious but obscure. Very simply, the idea of marketing is that a business ought, as far as possible, to start with its customers; and it should gear all its efforts to giving the customers what they want—at a profit, of course. This means, for example, that customers should somehow have some say in the design of the product; and that it should be made as easy as possible for the customer to buy.

What is marketing?

The process

The process of marketing, then, includes a whole range of activities relating to selling the product—actual selling, decisions on pricing and distribution policy, advertising and other forms of promotion—and, indeed, at least part of the specification of the product. It involves, therefore, the market research and intelligence on which the necessary understanding of the customer must be based. This collection of activities is usually called, in marketing jargon, the 'marketing mix'.

2 The marketing mix

two points of view

It is useful to look at the marketing mix from two points of view. The first is a simple, practical analysis of how it fits into the operations of the business. Bearing in mind that marketing should have contributed, through market research, to the specification of the product, it is easiest to see it as filling the time and space between when the product comes off the end of the production line and when the ultimate customer buys it. (In fact, if you are making a complex piece of machinery, or selling insurance, it goes beyond this, into after-sales service.)

(a) keeping down the cost

The businessman's task is to plan how best to fill the gap, in terms of making the best use of available resources to achieve sufficient sales, profitably, to satisfied customers.

If you look at the costs of a hypothetical manufacturing company, you will find a picture which looks, basically, rather like the one shown in Fig. 1.1.

1.	Value of sales		100
	Less		
	2. Cost of materials		35
	3. Labour and related costs		10
	4. Overheads		10
= 5.	Gross margin	45	
	Less		
	6. Selling and distribution costs		30
= 7.	Net profit (pre-tax)	15	

Fig. 1.1 P/L statement for hypothetical manufacturing company (£'000s)

To all intents and purposes, item 6 is the marketing mix in this simple trading statement. For the manager with a sales target to meet and a planned gross margin of 45 per cent, the problem is how to use as little as possible of that margin to achieve his sales target, and to have a continuing, viable business and, hence, to make a satisfactory profit.

(b) keeping the customer happy

The second way to look at the marketing mix is to consider what the mix is actually doing to the relationship between the product and its purchasers. In a way, the key to this lies in what I have just said. Most businesses are looking for continuing success. They achieve this, basically, through satisfied customers—and they have to do it in the face of their competitors.

3   Through the elements of the marketing mix, the business sets out to build and maintain its competitive position. In most cases, the most effective way to protect this position is through successfully *branding* its products. The distinction between a product and a brand is important, as it explains much of what marketing tries to do, and much of the use of advertisements.

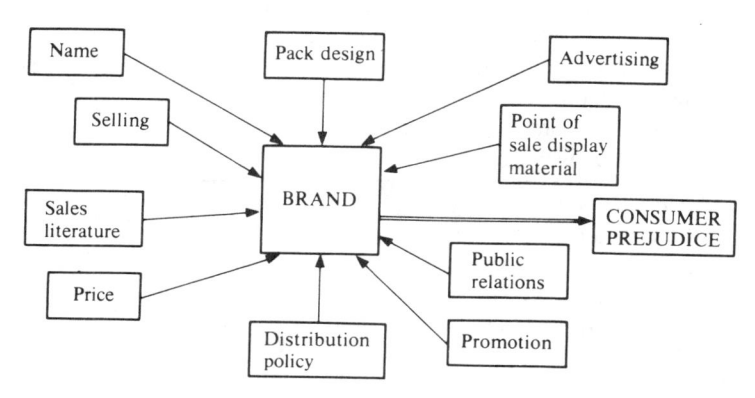

Fig. 1.2   How a brand fits together

A product, in these terms, is quite simply something which is offered to potential buyers and which, while it may be very good of its kind, is not systematically presented in a way which differentiates it from its competitors. A brand, on the other hand, is a product whose producer has set out deliberately and consistently to use every element in its presentation to make it uniquely desirable to its potential buyers. If this is done successfully, it makes the brand extremely difficult to compete with—not necessarily because it is physically that much better than its competitors, but because it has acquired an aura (a 'brand image') which makes it appear that much better.

4   A brand is created by all the elements in the marketing mix working together, consistently, to create a clear prejudice in its favour among its customers. In other words, a brand has a place in people's minds, as a brand, whereas a mere product is simply a way of fulfilling a physical need. In a competitive economy, there is a clear theoretical advantage in being a brand.

Diagrammatically, being a brand is quite a simple concept. All the parts of the marketing mix, as a consistent group, contribute their share to the product, so as to help build up a favourable prejudice among its actual and potential customers—roughly as shown in Fig. 1.2. Of course, it may not be necessary to use all the elements in the diagram to build up a particular brand. The possible combinations are numerous.

The role of advertising

How does advertising fit in with all this? Obviously, it can be one of the elements which contribute to the character and reputation of the brand. It can, clearly, be a very important part of getting to the customer, in order to create that favourable prejudice. Ultimately though, its role is, very simply, to sell: if it fails to do that, in one way or another, there is little point in it.

B. Check your understanding

Read through the text carefully, looking up anything you do not understand. Then answer the following questions.

1. Does the fact that it pays to advertise seem obvious to you? Explain your answer.
2. Do all businesses advertise?
3. Are there other ways, besides advertising, in which companies may persuade people to buy their products?
4. What sorts of resources does every business buy?
5. What does it do with them?

6. What does 'marketing' mean?
7. Is it the same thing as 'selling'?
8. What should marketing start with?
9. What should it give to the customers?
10. What does it expect in return?

11. What activities does marketing involve, apart from actual selling?
12. On what is the understanding of the customer based?
13. What is the first suggested way of looking at marketing mix?
14. From Figure 1.1, what are the two most costly items in the Profit and Loss statement?
15. What would be the effect on profit if the cost of advertising were increased without a rise in sales?

16. What is the manager's chief problem in ensuring that his business makes a viable profit?
17. What is the second suggested view of marketing mix?
18. What must a business have if it is to be continuously successful?
19. What is the difference between a non-branded product and a branded one?
20. What is the role of advertising?

C. Increase your vocabulary

Explain in your own words the meaning of the following, as used in the text:

- paragraph 1, line 20: jumped-up
  - 23: defensive
  - 26: ingenious but obscure

- paragraph 2, lines 8–9: after-sales service
  - 13: hypothetical

- Figure 1.1, line 6: gross margin
  - 9: net profit
  - pre-tax

- Figure 1.1, caption: P/L statement

- Figure 1.2: CONSUMER PREJUDICE

- paragraph 3, line 15: aura

- paragraph 4, line 17: favourable prejudice
  ultimately
  lines 18–19: in one way or another

What do you think would be the meaning of 'post-tax'?

D. Check your grammar

> **Remember**
> both . . . and . . .
> not only . . . but (also) . . .

e.g., (a) Advertising is expensive. Advertising is difficult to do well.
  (b) Advertising is both expensive and difficult to do well.
  (c) Advertising is not only expensive but also difficult to do well.

Now supply the other two forms for each of the following:

1. (a) It must improve sales. It must increase profit.
2. (b) Advertising must both please the customer and bring in more income.
3. (c) It must not only be visually attractive but also outshine the competition.
4. (a) A branded product will appear to be better. A branded product should actually be better.
5. (a) An advert must please people who do not yet use your brand. An advert must please people who already use your brand.

Is there any difference in meaning or emphasis between the different forms?

E. Understanding a lecture

Listen to the lecture on your tape in order to hear what it is all about. Then look at the questions below and play the tape again, section by section, and make notes for your answers. You can then write them up in complete sentences to form a summary of the argument.

1. Does it matter whether the effect of advertising is long-term or not?
2. What decision might rest on an answer to this question?
3. How long, in some people's opinion, must an advertising campaign last if the effect is not to disappear quickly?
4. Does the record of famous brand names support this opinion?
5. What does 'household names' mean?
6. What is the first reason the lecturer gives for the fact that some people believe the effect of advertising is long lasting?
7. What does payment 'over the odds' mean?
8. What is the second reason?
9. What do people think of when they are asked about Brooke Bond advertising?
10. What do Brooke Bond sell?

F. Understanding a printed text (2)

The economic task

1 The basic task of advertising, nine times out of ten, is to sell, or to assist sales.

It follows, therefore, that if you can sell all you want to without advertising, you can do without it—unless you can see a way whereby advertising can save you some other cost. Usually, a new advertising campaign for a previously unadvertised brand is a straightforward addition to costs. This means, very crudely, that such a campaign has to be capable of generating additional sales and, more precisely, marginal profits sufficient to cover the added costs. What is more, it ought to be capable of doing this more cheaply than any alternative method—such as adding another half dozen men to the sales force, or opening up a wholly new distribution channel.

The one very fundamental reason for advertising, then, is to sell more, more profitably. This is, however, a very typical example of advertising language, since it begs the question: 'More than what?'. Once you ask that question, the whole situation rapidly becomes rather complicated, instead of the apparently simple picture we have been looking at. If a brand has been on the market for some time, its sales may have started to decline: by means of advertising, the decline may be slowed. In this case, sales will be, say, 5 per cent down rather than the 10 per cent down which they would have been without the advertising. In other words, with advertising you will actually be selling *less*, but that 'less' is still more than the result which (you assume) would have been achieved without advertising—and this may be a major benefit to your overall profitability.

The roles of advertising

2 Clearly, in order to achieve these extra sales, advertising has to be working in some way in the marketplace. The market for a particular product consists, if you analyse it in detail, of a number of different groups of people, who can be categorized in terms of their relationship to the product:

Non-users of the product category
1. Those who do not and never will use these products.
2. Non-users who are possible future users but are unaware of our product.
3. Non-users who are possible future users and are aware of our product.

Users of the product category
1. Users of competitive brands, who are unaware of our product.
2. Users of competitive brands, who are aware of our product
   (a) Who have never tried our product.
   (b) Who have tried our product.
3. Users of both competitive brands and of our product.
4. Users of our product only
   (a) Who have never used another brand.
   (b) Who have used another brand.

Once you look at a market like this it becomes clear that the apparently simple task of using advertising to increase sales of our brand can be achieved by working against virtually any (or all) of the dozen or so different groups of people described. And to work against each of these groups the advertising may have to have a rather different effect: it can *remind* the brands' users to buy it—or to use it; it can try to *persuade* users of competitive brands that our brand is as good as or better than the one that they are using at present; it can *make aware* the ignorant about our brand's existence, and *inform* them about its virtues; it can, conceivably, *encourage* non-users to use the product category.

	1977 %	1978 %
Chesebrough-Ponds	8.3	8.7
Smith Kline	7.4	8.2
Unilever	10.7	8.0
Mars	6.5	7.2
General Foods	5.6	6.2
Seagram	3.6	5.3
Pillsbury	5.0	4.8
Kelloggs	4.6	4.7
Philip Morris	3.5	3.6
McDonalds	3.8	3.0
Colgate-Palmolive	3.1	2.8
Kraft	1.9	1.0
Greyhound	1.3	1.0
ITT	0.6	0.8

Figure 2.1   A/S ratios of some top US advertising spenders.
(Source: *Advertising Age*, 6 September 1979)

3 The simplest method—and the commonest—is to take a standard percentage of sales revenue as the basis for the budget. This has its basis, clearly, in the way in which products are costed, since it is quite easy to decide—even if only arbitrarily—that, given a particular level of gross margin, a certain proportion of this can be devoted to advertising.

Making a budget

This method of setting the budget, or 'appropriation', as it is usually called, has the virtue of simplicity. It is, however, obviously fairly naive, since it has no obvious relation to what is happening in the rest of the market, in terms of either the market's dynamics or competitive activity. In some cases, indeed, the budget is based on a set proportion of the previous year's sales, rather than of the forecast sales for the year being budgeted. In any market where things are changing at all rapidly, this seems to be, to say the least, an odd way to plan.

appropriation

The fact is that deciding on an advertising-to-sales ratio or 'A/S ratio' is far from easy, as it should depend both on the competitive character of the market and on the individual brand's position in the market. Numerous studies have shown clearly that A/S ratios vary quite markedly between different companies, different markets and different brands within markets. *Ad Age* has published a regular series of estimates of A/S ratios for a wide range of US markets which shows a marked variation between markets and some quite large changes in the A/S ratios of some markets over time (see Fig. 2.1.).

G. Check your understanding

Read through the text carefully, looking up anything you do not understand. Then answer the following questions:

1. What is the usual basic task of advertising?
2. What must advertising do in order to justify itself?
3. Does successful advertising necessarily mean a rise in sales?
4. Into what two main categories does the writer place potential customers?
5. What effect should good advertising have on the following sorts of people:
   - your own brand users?
   - users of competitive brands?
   - people who did not know that your brand existed?
   - people who do not use your sort of product?
6. What is the simplest way to calculate how much to spend on advertising?
7. What is the drawback of such a system of calculating?
8. Does Figure 2. show a general trend?

H. Understanding discourse

Imagine you are the MD of a small company about to enter the market with a new product. Listen to the tutor discussing on your tape the problem of deciding whether or not to advertise through an advertising agency. What three possible courses does he mention?

Now look at Figure 3.1 showing the advantages and disadvantages of these three courses. Then fill in the table underneath the figure, as the tutor instructs you, and make your decision. Be prepared to justify it.

	Agency	Specialist services	Do it yourself
Advantages	All-round skills All-round experience Objective outsider's point of view of your business You can learn from others' mistakes They do the whole job for you Continuity of work contact	You can pick the real experts for each part of the job You can fill the gaps in your capabilities, without having to buy the complete service of the agency May be cheaper May be faster	Everything in your control Full understanding of your problems Learn as you go along (no embarrassment at lack of knowledge) May be faster Probably cheaper
Disadvantages	Lack of specific knowledge of your business (usually) Cannot devote all their time to you May do a poor job for a small client Probably expensive to use	Need careful control and coordination: this needs experience Require extra careful briefing—every time Difficult to get extra services in a hurry	Easy to make mistakes—no one available to cross-check Lack of required skills Lack of specialized know-how Limited view—no outside knowledge to provide a different viewpoint or stimulus

Fig. 3.1 Advantages and disadvantages of the three ways of handling advertising

Factors	Questions	Answers	Decision
1			
2			
3			
4			
5			
6			

Overall decision:...............................

Table taken from WHITE, *Advertising: what it is and how to do it*, McGraw-Hill, 1980

UNIT 12 — PLANNING THE ATTACK

A. Understanding a printed text (1)

The following text discusses how to plan an advertising policy. Look at its structure, including the headings, illustration and caption. Then read through the passage quickly and find the answers to the following questions. Remember that you do not have to understand every word in order to do so.

1. What is the broad difference between marketing objectives and marketing strategies?
2. What does Figure 7.1 illustrate?

How ads are born

1 Advertisements do not usually spring fully formed into the mind of an agency's resident creative genius. Most advertisements, if they are any good, are the outcome of a process of careful, detailed and imaginative analysis, which leads to the formulation of an advertising strategy for the brand concerned. This strategy should be agreed in advance between agency and client, before any advertising ideas are put forward. If you are the client, you are, obviously, impatient to see some ideas. It is very tempting to go for the ideas and ignore the reasons for them. This is a mistake. If the strategy is not soundly based, there is every risk that what seems on the surface a good idea is, in fact, misdirected and misconceived. It is, therefore, essential to develop an appropriate strategy for the advertising before starting to produce ideas.

Objectives and strategies

2 At this stage, it is important to distinguish between a variety of different types of 'objective', or 'strategy', or 'intention', or 'role' for advertising. People in marketing have a tendency to use confusing language and, in consequence, to set up requirements which, logically, cannot be met.

Marketing

Marketing *objectives* are specific targets set in terms of sales, brand share, distribution, consumer penetration, re-purchase, etc.
Marketing *strategy* is the statement of the means by which the objectives can be achieved. These means may (or may not) include advertising, as a major or minor element within the total marketing mix.

Advertising

The *role* of advertising within the marketing mix is the part it has to play in the marketing strategy. Because advertising is not the only element in the overall marketing mix .... advertising's role is almost certainly going to be to meet part only of the marketing strategy. This may be anything from increasing brand awareness to improving specific aspects of the brand image.
Advertising *objectives* are more or less specific statements of what is to be achieved by advertising, in terms of (for example) increased awareness, or improved scores on certain attitude scales.
Advertising *strategy* is a statement of how the objectives are to be achieved, in terms of creative content and media deployment.
For the creative department of the agency, then, there are specific creative objectives, to be achieved through the fulfilment of creative strategy.

Developing the strategy

3   The ultimate aim of the advertising planner is to develop an advertising strategy which provides the answers to two superficially straightforward questions:

- Who do we want to talk to?
- What do we want them to get out of our advertising?

In order to arrive at the answer, he needs to go through a more or less logical process of analysis, based on market research—whether published, or commissioned by the client, or (occasionally) commissioned by the agency—and on his knowledge and experience.

What he needs to know can be set out in the form of a cycle of information and analysis—a cycle, because marketing and advertising are a continuous process, and knowledge gained from one advertising campaign can be used to develop its continuation. The cycle can look like that shown in Fig. 7.1.

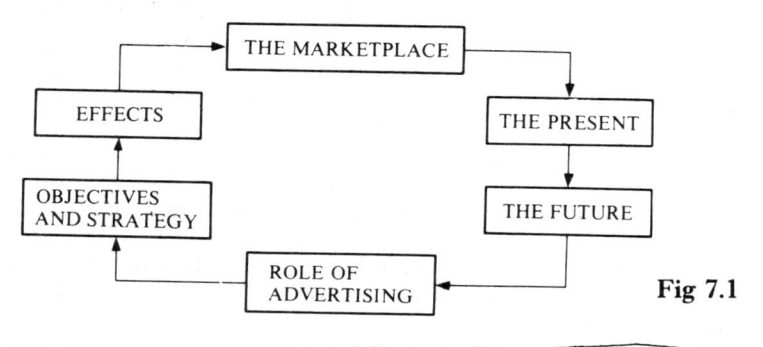

```
            THE MARKETPLACE
           ↗              ↘
     EFFECTS            THE PRESENT
        ↑                   ↓
   OBJECTIVES           THE FUTURE
   AND STRATEGY            ↓
        ↖              ↙
         ROLE OF
         ADVERTISING
```

Fig 7.1

4   Different agencies use rather different versions of this, but they all look broadly similar.

The terms used in this version cover the following general areas:

The marketplace

The market in which our brand competes: trends in sales, consumption, distribution; the state of product development; the level of competitive advertising and promotional activity; patterns of consumption—are there heavy or light users of the products and who are they?

The present

This sets out to describe the client's position within the marketplace: brand shares and trends in brand share; product advantages and disadvantages over competition—both in physical terms (laboratory test and blind consumer test) and in terms of consumer opinions and attitudes; planned and possible product improvements; recent marketing activity, in relation to that of competitors.

The future

This reflects, primarily, the client's objectives for the brand—what are his targets, in terms of sales, market share, consumer purchasing and usage? But to these targets needs to be added an analysis of what must be achieved in order to obtain them, in terms of both the behaviour and attitude of consumers: and of more functional matters such as (for example) greatly improved distribution—to put it in what is, from the agency's point of view, the most defensive way possible, it is too easy to blame the advertising when the sales force has failed to achieve the necessary levels of retail distribution to support the required sales.

(d)

Advertising objectives and strategy

In practice, one should here consider *all* the different forms of communication of the product to the consumer, and allocate to each, and to sales activity, product development, market research, etc., their specific roles in meeting the objectives. For example, although most retail grocery advertising in the UK seems to consist of lists of prices, and consumers tend to expect it to do so, it seems unrealistic to expect advertising to do the major job of communicating large numbers of prices, especially promotional prices, when this can be done far better by window bills and in-store display: there are few shoppers who analyse every available grocery ad before deciding where to shop. Surely the role of advertising for a grocery chain is to give customers good reasons other than price for shopping there.

Thus, it is possible to define the role of advertising for a product or brand as being (for example):

- to maintain the loyalty of existing buyers, and to encourage them to use more;
- to encourage non-users to sample the product;
- to inform consumers, especially lapsed users, that the product has been improved or reformulated;
- to develop the belief among both users and, ideally, non-users that the brand is technically superior to competitors for reasons A, B or C;
- to increase awareness of the brand and its characteristics.

On the basis of this analysis, it is possible to develop specific objectives and creative and media strategies for the advertising. I will come back to this in a moment.

The effect

Presumably, the advertising will have some effect on the market. It is an essential element in the planning cycle to measure the effects of the advertising, as far as possible, together with those of other types of marketing activity, in order to take account of what has happened in the next phase of planning.

B. Check your understanding

Read through the passage carefully, looking up anything you do not understand. Then answer the following questions.

1. Does an advertising agency immediately produce a fully formed advertisement?
2. What process usually precedes the formulation of an advertising strategy?
3. What comes first, ideas or strategy?
4. What risk is involved in adopting the wrong strategy?
5. Is advertising necessarily a part of a marketing strategy?
6. Why is Figure 7.1 called a cycle?

C. Increase your vocabulary

Explain in your own words the meaning of the following as used in the text:

- paragraph 1, line 2: resident creative genius
            10: misdirected
      lines 10–11: misconceived

- paragraph 2, line 6: consumer penetration
            9: major or minor element
            18: attitude scales

- paragraph 3, line 8: commissioned

- paragraph 4(a), line 4: heavy or light users
      (d), line 15: maintain the loyalty of existing users
            18: lapsed users

D. Check your grammar

Find the following words in the text and say what they refer to

- paragraph 2, line 10: it
            14: this

- paragraph 3, line 5: them
            6: he
            9: his
            13: its

- paragraph 4 (a), line 4: they
      (b)   6: that
      (c)   2: his

E. Understanding a lecture

Play through the lecture on creativity on your tape, to find out what it is all about. Then look at the questions below and play the tape again, section by section, making notes for your answers. You can then expand these into full sentences and make a summary of the argument.

1. Is it possible to tell someone how to create an advertisement?
2. Does the name of the product have to appear in it?
3. What is the basic element in a good ad?
4. Is an imaginative idea all that is needed?
5. What sort of idea is worth its weight in gold?
6. What is needed as well as a creative idea?

7. What can the best creators do?
8. Can most members of advertising agencies do this?
9. What do 'flashy' and 'trendy' mean?
10. How long does the effect of such ads last?

F. Understanding a printed text (2)

Judging advertisements

1 There are, though, three or four fundamental criteria for judging advertisements which can be applied more or less universally. These are:

- Does the ad make me stop and look at it?
- Is there an original or unusual idea in it?
- Does it work as a piece of design?
- Is it relevant to the product?
- Is it easy to understand?

These are all questions which can be asked—and answered—without knowledge of the purpose behind the advertisement. However, the critical questions are specific to the particular ad, and they are the ones that really matter. They are:

- Does this advertisement fit the strategy?
- Will it work?

It is only the answers to these questions that can really enable you to judge an ad, although it will certainly be good supporting evidence if the answers to the earlier questions are favourable. Basically, you can assess ads at two stages: before or after they have been run in the media —('pre-testing' and 'post-testing').

Pre-testing advertisements and strategy

2 It has already been pointed out that one of the reasons for setting an advertising strategy is to assess the effectiveness of the advertisement. Advertising must be designed to communicate certain ideas to certain types of people. It does not matter if it communicates totally different ideas to different types of people. This is not relevant. So when the Chairman's wife says she does not like it, or that she cannot understand it—or that she never sees your advertising—and your advertising is designed to appeal (say) to factory foremen or teenage girls, you can treat her judgement with the appropriate degree of contempt.

What has to be done, then, to discover whether the advertisement is in line with the strategy, almost inevitably involves a form of cheating. The simplest way of getting an answer is to show the advertisement to a number of individuals selected from the target group, or to a group of them, and to get a discussion going about the ad. This needs to be done skillfully, and is usually done by trained researchers, who are adept at getting people to talk and at avoiding asking leading questions—because that is not merely cheating, it will lead to your deluding yourself: in this type of interview people are only too eager to tell you what you want to know.

3   From this kind of research, you can find out a great deal about your ad and your product. The sort of questions it can answer are, for example: *sample questions*

   - Is the ad interesting?
   - Is the ad intelligible?
   - Is it liked or disliked? (It is not disastrous if it is disliked, but there need to be very strong compensating factors.)
   - What does it tell them about the product? What will it taste or smell like? What will it cost? Is that good value?
   - Do they believe this, or question it?
   - Who do they think the product will appeal to? What sort of people will use it? In what circumstances?
   - What sort of shops will sell the product?
   - What kind of feelings do they get from the ad—cheerful, serious, sad, confident . . . ?
   - Might they try the product? Or try it again?

4   What this sort of research will not have told you is anything about the advertising's ability to stand out and attract attention when it appears in the chosen media. This is something that you may feel a need to be sure of, and it is quite possible to devise tests which will give at least a good indication of the likely impact of the ad in these terms. *testing advertising*

   There is, however, a theoretical problem. It is perfectly true that an ad is useless if no one notices it. But it is by no means true that an ad which everyone notices is necessarily good—it may be noticed for reasons which are totally irrelevant to the strategy. And, furthermore, the ways in which people take in messages from ads are often almost subconscious. (This is not to say that you can deliberately reach people by advertising 'subliminally', merely that it is quite possible to get a message out of an ad without really being aware of it.)

5   The obvious test for an advertisement is 'Does it sell?' (or 'Does it sell more?'). Unfortunately, it is very rarely that this question can be answered precisely. It is unusual, except in the case of direct response or direct mail, for the advertising to be the only influence affecting sales. And even when it appears to be so, the level of sales is in itself a quite complex measure. It is easy, for example, to say that an advertising campaign failed to increase sales. But it may have succeeded magnificently in preventing sales from falling. *testing*

▼

G. Check your understanding

Read through the text carefully, looking up anything you do not understand. Then say if the following statements are correct or not:

- There are no universal criteria for judging advertisements. ☐
- To judge the originality of an ad, you must first know its purpose. ☐
- One of the critical questions about any ad is whether or not it fits the marketing strategy. ☐
- One of the purposes of a strategy is to enable one to make a judgement of the effectiveness of an ad. ☐
- It is a matter of great importance if an ad means different things to different people. ☐
- People you interview about the effectiveness of ads always try to tell you what they think you would like to hear. ☐
- It does not necessarily matter if people do not like an ad. ☐
- It matters very much if no one notices an ad. ☐
- Part of the influence of an advertisement is exerted on the customer's subconscious. ☐
- The best way to judge an ad is by its effect on sales, but this is in fact very difficult to do. ☐

H. Understanding discourse

Look at the table below, listen to the tutor discussing it on your tape, and note down your answers to the questions he asks.

OPINIONS OF DIFFERENT MEDIA

	Local evening paper %	National morning paper %	TV %	Magazines %
Helpful in day-to-day life?	34	33	32	9
Helpful in deciding what to buy?	34	12	23	20
Helpful in deciding where to buy things?	44	11	20	12
Media in which advertising is most interesting?	27	9	30	11
Media in which advertising is most useful?	36	8	15	11
Media in which one finds ads one can trust?	30	7	15	8

Table taken from WHITE, *Advertising: what it is and how to do it.* McGraw-Hill, 1980

The passages in sections A and F of this unit were taken (edited) from WHITE, *Advertising: what it is and how to do it.* McGraw-Hill, 1980

USING COMPUTERS (1)

UNIT 13

A. Understanding a printed text (1)

The following passage introduces the topic of **computers** and their uses in running a business office. Look at the way it is structured, and at the headings, illustration and caption. Then read it through quickly and look for the answers to the following questions. Remember, you do not have to understand every word in order to do so:

1. Why are computers now so widely used in offices?
2. Do you have to know all about the theory of computing in order to use a microcomputer?
3. What are the basic components of a microcomputer system?

Almost every medium-sized or large company will use computers to help run the office... ... ... you will probably have to work with a computer in your day-to-day duties, so you will need to know something about computers and the way they are used. A computer really does make office life easier because it can do all sorts of different jobs.

The same computer could be used, for example, as a word processor, for filing, printing invoices, working out statistics for the accounts department, and communicating with other offices. What it does depends on the *program*, the long list of instructions by which the programmer tells it what to do.

When a company decides to install a computer (of any size), it usually gets a *systems analyst* to study the ways in which the machine might best be used. If the company is a large one, the systems analyst may be a full-time employee, looking after the continuous improvement and adaptation of the computer system. The systems analyst will recommend what kinds of program and computer equipment are required.

Programming is for experts. Computer programs are written in *languages* with names that are usually abbreviations or acronyms: Cobol (COmmon Business Oriented Language), RPG (Report Program Generator), Fortran (FORmula TRANslator), BASIC (Beginners' All-purpose Symbolic Instruction Code). This is of passing interest only, as the user of the computer in an office will have no way of knowing what programming language was used.

Many companies buy ready-written programs 'off the shelf', or buy programs that can be tailored to specific needs but are mostly standard. This reduces the cost of the system, for programming is very expensive and time-consuming. Once it is installed

**11.1
Why use
computers?**

programs

**11.2
Systems analysis**

systems analyst

**11.3
Computer
programming**

computer languages

and running, a well-designed computer system can take over much of the routine (and boring) work and at the same time provide accurate information about the business quickly and efficiently.

11.4 Types of computer

Computers in the office can be divided broadly into two categories:

(a) Mainframe and minicomputers
(b) Microcomputers

Computers are classified according to their size, power, and type of processing unit. The most powerful type of computer is the *mainframe computer*. Only large companies are likely to use a mainframe computer, as these machines are very expensive to buy and run.

mainframe

A *minicomputer* is the next size down, a sort of 'small mainframe'. It is a slower, less powerful version of the same class of computer, and is designed for businesses who do not need (or cannot afford) the capacity and speed of the smallest mainframe.

minicomputer

The smallest type of computer is the *microcomputer*. The name derives not from the small size of the machine—although the largest microcomputer can fit comfortably on a desk—but from the fact that the main processing circuits are on a single silicon chip, known as a *microprocessor*.

microcomputer

microprocessor

From the office worker's point of view the main difference between the two categories is that of location: mainframe and minicomputers require their own special room, often air-conditioned, and trained computer staff to operate them, whereas microcomputers can be found dotted round the building wherever there is a need for one.

11.5 All you need to know about the way computers work

CPU
RAM

Despite the differences in size, all computers work on the same principles, and all have the same kind of internal organization. At the heart of the computer is the *central processing unit* (CPU). The CPU is connected to the computer's *random access memory* (RAM). The RAM is an electronic system for storing information, either numbers or letters, and then subsequently retrieving it. To visualize the RAM, think of an enormous array of thousands of little boxes, each one with a numbered lid so the computer can find it. The computer can go to any of the boxes, and either place a number or letter inside or read the value of an existing number or letter.

byte

Each memory location (each box) represents the smallest item of information the computer can handle, called a *byte*. The number of bytes available is a measure of the size of the RAM. The RAM is used to contain two separate kinds of information: the information that is being processed and the program.

The computer is no use at all if it cannot communicate with the outside world, so it is fitted with *input* and *output* devices. The most common input device is the familiar QWERTY *keyboard*, and the most common output devices are the even more familiar TV screen, known in computer circles as a *monitor* or *Visual Display Unit* (VDU), and the *printer*. Details of other input and output devices are given below, but one is worth a mention at this stage as it is a vital part of the system: the *backing store*. When the power is turned off, the RAM loses its memory. It is therefore essential to have some means of keeping a permanent electronic record. Although recording tape is sometimes used, the computer *disk* is the usual way. The disk varies in size, form and cost, according to the type of machine, but it is basically a cross between a gramophone record and a tape. The surface is coated with magnetic oxide, like a recording tape, and a pick-up arm fitted with a magnetic head either records or plays back the disk. A disk can hold from 100 kilobytes to scores of megabytes, according to size and type. It is preferable to a tape, in the same way that a gramophone record is better than a tape—you can choose any track and play it, without having to wind through the whole thing. A disk drive as fitted to a microcomputer would have an *access time* (the time it takes to find any given item of information) of a few thousandths of a second. If that seems fast, getting information from the RAM would take less than a millionth of a second (see Unit 14).

The program for the computer will be recorded on the disk, and before anything else can happen, the program (or parts of it) must be 'read in' to the RAM. Once it has its instructions, the computer can set about its task, which may also involve looking at (or accessing) the disk for data or for more program.

So to start up a computer, the sequence will always be roughly the same: turn it on; load the program into RAM from the disk or tape; start work.

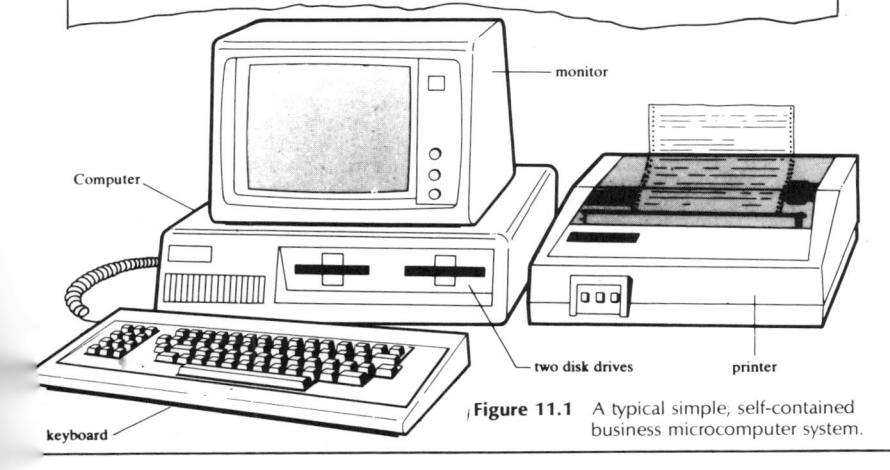

input and output
keyboard

VDU
printer

disks

access time

Figure 11.1 A typical simple, self-contained business microcomputer system.

11.6 Practical office systems: The microcomputer

disk drive

operating system

In practice, the office computer system may appear to be more complicated. We can start by looking at a typical microcomputer, which might be used for word processing and filing.

The system is illustrated in Figure 11.1 and consists of the *computer*, fitted with two *disk drives*, a *monitor*, and a *printer*. Switch on. The computer, disk drive and printer may all have separate switches. Find the program disk. Microcomputers generally use 5¼- or 3½-inch disks, which are protected by a square plastic sleeve or pack. Make sure the disk goes in the right way. A couple of keys, or sometimes a simple typed instruction, will get the disk to load. From there on, the program takes over. In some cases, the computer may require two programs. The first of these is called the *operating system*. Operating systems have names like CP/M, Unix and MS-DOS. The operating system is really just a program that tells the computer how to control the disk drive, printer, and whatever else is attached. After the operating system is loaded, the main program, which may be on a separate disk, can go in.

Once the program starts up, the screen will tell you what to do. Some programs are more obscure than others. One may say 'Put data disk in drive 2', another may say 'I/O D2?' which may require a look at the instruction manual for translation. Programs are getting better—more 'user-friendly' in this respect.

Word processing programs are generally easy to use, and the best way to get acquainted is to take an hour or two to find your way round it. It is impossible to harm the computer by pressing the wrong keys. Sometimes microcomputers are linked together in what is called a network. This is explained in more detail below (see Unit 14F).

B. Check your understanding

Read through the text carefully, looking up anything you do not understand. Then answer the following questions.

1. How does a computer make office life easier?
2. What determines what a computer does?
3. What is a program?
4. Who decides what sort of equipment to instal?
5. Do you need to know which language a computer uses before you can work with it?
6. What is the advantage of using ready-made programs?
7. How are computers classified?
8. What is the difference between a mainframe computer and a minicomputer?
9. How does the microcomputer get this name?
10. Where is a microcomputer most used?
11. Are all kinds of computers based on the same principles?
12. What is the function of RAM?
13. What do you call the smallest piece of information a computer can handle?
14. How do you measure RAM?
15. What is a computer screen called? What is the common abbreviation?
16. What happens to RAM when a computer's power is switched off?
17. What do you use in order to keep a permanent record?
18. What are the two basic uses of a microcomputer in an ordinary office?
19. What do you think 'user-friendly' means?
20. What do a number of linked microcomputers form?

C. Increase your vocabulary

Computer users tend to speak a language all their own! The following are computer terms occurring in this passage and in passage F of this unit, plus a few others necessary for understanding them:

PASSAGE A

access time:	the length of time it takes a computer to obtain information from a storage device or *primary memory*
backing store:	a data storage medium other than primary memory
bit:	a contraction of Binary digIT — a single binary digit, either 0 or 1
byte:	eight *bits*, the smallest item of information used by most computers
Central Processing Unit (CPU):	the computer itself, without any *peripherals*
cursor:	a flashing symbol on the *monitor* screen, to show where something is expected to happen
disk (diskette):	a random access storage device, using a metal or plastic disk coated in magnetic oxide (NB American spelling)
input device:	anything that feeds information (e.g., keyboard, *modem*, *bar-code* reader)
mainframe computer:	the most powerful class of computer

microcomputer:		the cheapest class of computer, having the main part of its electronics on a single silicon chip (microprocessor)
minicomputer:		a class of computer one step down from a *mainframe*
monitor:		a screen like that of a TV, but giving a sharper picture, used in computer systems to display information for the user (also known as *Visual Display Unit (VDU)*.)
operating system:		the software (*disks*, etc.) used by a computer to control the system
primary memory:		the electronic memory in which the computer stores the program and the data on which it is currently working
Random Access Memory (RAM):		See *primary memory*
Visual Display Unit (VDU):		See *monitor*

PASSAGE F

line printer:	high speed printer
menu:	a list of options presented on the *monitor*, enabling the user to select the one required
password:	a secret word or number that is typed into the computer at the appropriate time, to allow the user access to information which is restricted.
terminal:	a *monitor* and a keyboard (and sometimes a printer) connected to a *network* or directly to a *mainframe* or a *minicomputer* serving more than one user

NB: further terms are given in section C of Unit 14.

D. Check your grammar

Look at the following timetable of lectures

	MON	TUES	WED	THURS	FRI
09.00	Mr Smouth CASH FLOW	Mr Clarke ACCOUNTANCY	P R	Mr Smouth CASH FLOW	Miss Goode SALES
10.15	Mr Trend DESIGN	Miss Prince COMPUTERS	O J E	Mr Flash ADVERTISING	Mr Trend DESIGN
11.15	Mr Flash ADVERTISING	Miss Goode SALES	C T	Miss Prince COMPUTERS	Mr Clarke ACCOUNTANCY

Remember your tenses

- Has Mr Trend given his lecture on design yet?
  Yes, he gave it on Monday.

- Did you go to Mr Clarke's lecture on accountancy?
  No, but I'm going to one on Friday.

- Will there be any more lectures on sales?
  Yes, there's one on Friday.

Now, imagine it is Wednesday afternoon, and a new student has just joined the course. He asks you questions about the timetable, using the above models, and you give answers. Working with another student if possible, make short dialogues in this way. You may use 'yesterday' and 'tomorrow' where appropriate, instead of naming a day.

E. Understanding a lecture

Listen to the lecture on your tape about computer language. Play it through as many times as necessary for you to note down definitions of the following ten terms:
- databank
- create
- merge
- archive
- delete
- locate
- send
- lock
- retrieve
- database

F. Understanding a printed text (2)

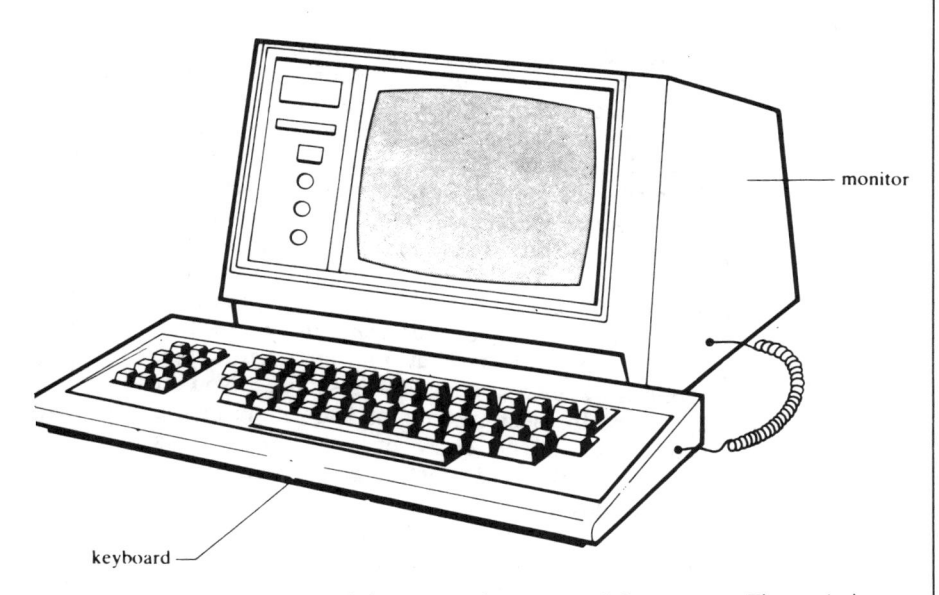

ure 11.2 A typical terminal for a mainframe or minicomputer. The switches next to the screen control communications with the computer.

If you are working for a big company then you will probably be using a mainframe computer. In business, the mainframe computer will almost certainly be serving more than one *terminal*, and quite possibly several printers. The mainframe computer itself (take this whole section to refer to minicomputers, too) will live in its own room, probably air-

**11.7
Practical office systems:
The mainframe computer**

terminal

conditioned to keep it at exactly the most favourable temperature. The room may well have a filtered air supply, to exclude dust as far as possible. The computer and its backing store will take up quite a lot of room. Most mainframe and minicomputers use hard disk storage, and each of these storage units takes up as much space as a small desk. Whereas the microcomputer uses a printer that is not too far removed from the office electronic typewriter, the mainframe computer may well drive a *line printer*, capable of printing thousands of lines of print per minute. Such printers are too large and noisy to go into the average office, and will probably be located in the computer room.

line printer

Unless you work in the computer department as a computer operator, you will never have to visit the computer room to use the machine.

Because it is so fast and powerful, the mainframe computer can cope with simultaneous input from many terminals. Each terminal will have a screen and a keyboard; a typical example is illustrated in Figure 11.2.

Using a terminal is not very different from using a microcomputer. Everything is controlled by the program (computer experts sometimes call programs 'software', as opposed to the machines which are called 'hardware'). What appears on the screens of the terminals depends on the type of business, the type of computer, and the application. Terminals can be used for entry of orders, inputting daily information about stocks and customers, accounts, almost anything. But instead of putting in your own program disk as you do when using the microcomputer, you simply select what you want from a range of options—known as a *menu*—presented to you on the screen. In most systems at least some of the options require the entry of a *password*. This prevents unauthorized people changing critical data such as salaries.

software
hardware

menu

Sometimes a terminal will have its own printer, but often if you want something printed out you can ask for it with the terminal, but the actual printing is done by the line printer in the computer department.

Large laser printers are found in computer rooms. They are very fast and handle large volumes of work. Information from the computer—text, graphics, format and fonts required—is assembled by the printer into images, which are written by laser beam on to a light-sensitive drum.

Printing is silent, a page at a time.

G. Check your understanding

Read through the passage carefully, looking up anything you do not understand. Then say whether the following statements are correct or not:
1. Mainframe computers are used by large companies. ☐
2. Each computer serves a number of terminals. ☐
3. There is only one printer per computer. ☐
4. A mainframe computer has to be separately housed in a room of its own. ☐
5. A mainframe computer is large and makes a lot of noise. ☐
6. Each mainframe terminal has its own VDU. ☐
7. Using a mainframe terminal is very different from using a desk-top microcomputer screen. ☐
8. When you use a mainframe terminal, you do not have your own disk. ☐
9. Mainframe terminals do not have their own printers. ☐
10. Laser printing is a very noisy process. ☐

H. Understanding discourse

Listen to the tutor talking on your tape about floppy disks. Look at the drawing below as he talks. Then label the drawing and answer the questions on the next page, first in note form and then as a summary of what the tutor says.

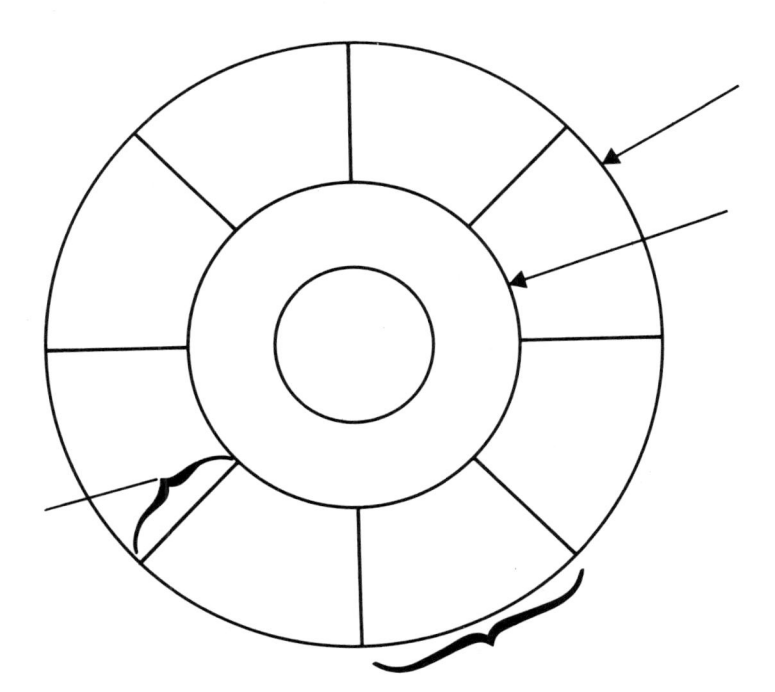

- How does a floppy disk compare with a long-playing gramophone record?
- How does the technology differ in the various kinds of floppy disk?
- How does a disk drive write?
- Why do disks have to be handled so carefully?
- What is the advantage of having two read/write heads?
- What determines the number of tracks on a disk?
- What is the advantage of having more tracks?
- What is the disadvantage?
- How many sectors are there on a disk?
- Why are disks from one system incompatible with another?

The passages in this unit and in Unit 14 were taken (edited) from TROTMAN, *Modern Secretarial Procedures*, McGraw-Hill, 1986

USING COMPUTERS (2)

UNIT 14

A. Understanding a printed text (1)

The following text continues the topic of using computers in the office, concentrating this time on **computer peripherals**. Look first at the general structure of the passage and at the marginal notes and the headings. Then look at the following questions and read through the text quickly to find the answers.

1. What is meant by peripherals?
2. What is the general difference between the various kinds of disk?
3. In what basic way do the various printers differ from each other?

Already, you will have realized that there are lots of different input and output devices that can be connected to the computer. Such devices are known collectively as computer *peripherals*, and the following sections give a summary of some of the more important ones that you are likely to meet. The first range of devices to consider are backing stores.

(a) Disks

Disks come in a range of sizes. Three types are popular for microcomputers. The most common is the 5¼-inch floppy disk (or diskette, or flexible disk, or just 'floppy'). The disk is protected by a square plastic sleeve, which is not removed: there is a slot that lets the machine get at the disk's surface. Disks of all kinds are delicate. DON'T touch the surface of the disk, bend it, or smoke while using it. The 5¼-inch disk holds between 100 and 800 kilobytes.

Second in popularity is the 3½-inch disk, sometimes called a *microdisk*. This is built into a rigid plastic protective box with a cover that slides back when you put the disk into the machine. These disks have about the same capacity as the 5¼-inch versions.

Third is the *Winchester* disk. This is a very different kind of disk storage system. There is only one disk, permanently built into a special cabinet about the size of a video recorder. Although you can't replace the disk in a Winchester system, the disk has such a large capacity—several megabytes (millions of bytes)—that it is not really a problem. The Winchester disk has a very fast access time.

There is actually another type of floppy disk, the 8-inch disk, but these are becoming less common as the performance of the smaller types improves.

**11.8
Computer peripherals:
Backing stores**

floppy disks

microdisk

Winchester disk

back-up disk

formatting

All disks, even the Winchester, are prone to failure from time to time. Floppy disks in particular will become worn, and the computer will suddenly decide that it can no longer read them. It is therefore wise to make copies of disks (known as *back-up disks*) at regular intervals when you are typing data into a microcomputer. Always be aware that a disk fault, or even a brief power failure, will lose all the work you have typed in, from the point when you last made a back-up. Almost all microcomputers have two disk drives, so you can put a blank disk in one slot and the full disk in the other to copy it.

It is worth mentioning briefly that you cannot use a new floppy disk straight out of the pack. It has to be *formatted*. Formatting is nothing more complicated than putting the disk in the computer and typing in the right instruction. The computer checks the disk is undamaged, and records various things on it so that it can be used. A disk formatted in one computer will not necessarily work with a computer of a different make.

The various forms of hard disks and other storage devices used in the computer department will not form part of the secretary's work. It is enough to know that they are very fast, hold enormous amounts of information, and are very expensive.

(b) Tapes

Some microcomputers use cassette tapes for storing programs and data. Tapes can hold a lot of information, but are much slower to use than disks. In the computer department they may have huge tapes on reels. These store very large amounts of data, but suffer from the usual tape problem of long access times if the information you want is at the other end.

The disk and the RAM share a characteristic in that they are both random access storage devices. The computer can go immediately to any of the recorded data. A tape, on the other hand, is a serial access device from which information can be retrieved only in the order in which it was recorded.

11.9 Computer peripherals: Printers

daisy wheel

If you are using a microcomputer with a printer in the office, or have a printer attached to the terminal you are using, then it is probably one of two types, a daisy wheel printer or a matrix printer.

The *daisy wheel printer* uses a mechanism that is practically identical to that used by an ordinary electronic typewriter. The daisy wheel is a plastic wheel with 'petals' like a daisy. Each petal has a raised letter of the alphabet on the end. When the printer is working, the daisy wheel spins to bring the required letter to the top, then a mechanism bangs the petal forward on an ordinary typewriter ribbon, to print the letter on the paper.

Daisy wheel printers produce type that looks exactly as if it had been typed on a good typewriter, and are ideal for word processors or other applications where the best quality is needed. They are not, as such things go, particularly fast. The average is six to fifteen characters per second.

The second kind is the *matrix printer*. This is much faster than the daisy wheel, typically printing a line a second. The print does not look as if it has been done on a typewriter, so matrix printers are not often used for word processing. To produce characters, the matrix printer has a little block, the size of a letter, containing a matrix of 5×7 or 7×9 tiny needles. The character is formed by hitting the ribbon with selected needles forming the shape of the required letter. The letter is therefore made up of little dots, which are visible on a close look.

matrix printer

The matrix printer can also be used to do simple drawings, since the needles in the matrix can be operated individually by the computer; *computer graphics* such as pie charts, graphs and histograms can be printed out by suitable statistics programs.

computer graphics

Both the daisy wheel and matrix printer can be fitted with a normal typewriter-style *friction feed* for individual sheets of paper, a *tractor feed* for continuous lengths of computer paper (it has sprocket-holes down the edges), or a *sheet feed* for automatically feeding sheet after sheet of typing paper. *Continuous stationery*, as computer paper is called, is perforated so that it folds neatly and can be torn up into individual sheets. The sprocket holes are engaged by the tractor feed so that each 'sheet' is registered in exactly the right position in the printer.

friction feed
tractor feed

sheet feed

continuous stationery

There are many other types of printer, all much less common than these two. Perhaps the next most popular are *thermal printers*. These work in more or less the same way as matrix printers but have no ribbon. Instead, the needles of the matrix blacken special heat-sensitive paper by heating up. Thermal printers are fast and very quiet, but the paper is expensive. (See also **7.6** *(g)* (iv).)

thermal printers

Ink-jet printers use static electricity to direct tiny ink droplets onto the page. They are fast, silent, and produce good quality printing. On the debit side they are expensive and require more maintenance than the others.

ink-jet printers

11.10 Computer peripherals: Input devices

function keys

(a) Keyboard

The computer keyboard is similar in layout to a typewriter keyboard, but may have extra keys. Just as with typewriters, the layout differs from make to make. The most usual extra keys are *function keys*. These are generally marked F1, F2, etc., and can be used for different purposes in different programs. The keyboard is generally connected to the computer by a flexible cable. Small computers may have all the electronics built into the keyboard casing.

(b) Joystick

A control stick is sometimes used to supplement the keyboard. It is used to move something, generally a cursor, about the screen. The cursor is a flashing square or arrow that is used to point to something on the screen of the monitor. For example, you might select an item from the menu by moving the cursor against it and pressing the 'fire' button on the joystick.

(c) Mouse

A mouse is an improvement on the joystick. Instead of a control stick, you have a small plastic box on the desk in front of you. To move the cursor, you just move the mouse in the appropriate direction, across the desk, and the cursor follows. This is a more natural action than using the joystick. The mouse has one or two 'fire' buttons on its back.

(d) Touch-screen

Some monitors are built with a system that can detect where a finger is placed on the screen. You can select menu items simply by touching the appropriate part of the screen.

(e) Bar-code reader

Anyone who shops in a modern supermarket will be familiar with bar-code readers. The reader is a pen-shaped device that is plugged into the computer. At the tip of the reader is an optical sensor that detects printed marks. Moving the bar-code reader smoothly across an appropriate bar code (there is one on the back cover of this book) reads a number directly into the computer. Bar codes are widely used in stock control and other applications where lots of items have to be checked.

In addition to those listed above there are many other specialized input devices. Computer input can be from *punched cards* (becoming obsolete), *magnetic strips* (like the one on a credit card), *magnetic ink* (look at the numbers along the bottom of a cheque), or even typewriting. A special machine can be used to read a page of type into the computer—the technique is called optical character recognition (OCR).

punched cards
magnetic strips
magnetic ink

OCR

A portable microcomputer, intended for executives. It combines computer, printer, and a small monitor in a package small enough to fit into a briefcase. It can be linked to a network when in the office. (Courtesy of the Sharp Corporation)

Passage and illustration taken from TROTMAN, *Modern Secretarial Procedures*, McGraw-Hill, 1986

B. Check your understanding

Read through the text carefully, looking up anything you do not understand. Then answer the following questions:

1. What is a backing store?
2. What is the most popular form of backing store?
3. What must you avoid doing when you are using a floppy disk?
4. Why should you make back-up disks?
5. How do you format a disk?
6. What is the size of a microdisk?
7. Can you use a formatted disk in any kind of computer?
8. What is the drawback of computer tapes?
9. What have RAM and disks got in common?
10. Can a tape retrieve information in any order you wish?
11. What types of printer do microcomputers usually have?
12. Why is a daisy wheel so called?
13. What is it best used for?
14. How fast does it print?
15. What is the advantage of a matrix printer?
16. Is it used in word processing?
17. How does it work?
18. What sort of graphics can you print with it?
19. How is the paper fed in?
20. How does a thermal printer differ from a matrix printer?
21. What is a cursor?
22. How do you control a cursor?
23. What detects the message in a bar-code?
24. What are bar-codes used for?
25. What is the most common use of a magnetic strip?

C. Increase your vocabulary

The following are additional computer terms frequently in use (see also section C, Unit 13):

back-up disk: a copy of a disk made as a precaution in case the disk currently in use should become defective or damaged

continuous stationery: computer paper made in continuous length with the join between sheets perforated

daisy wheel printer: a printer with a mechanism similar to that of an electronic typewriter

friction feed: paper fed into a *printer* in the same way as a typewriter

formatting: preparing a *disk* for use. The computer must check the disk and record various pieces of information on it before the disk can be used for data storage

function keys: extra keys on a computer keyboard: their function depends on the program being used

ink-jet printer:	a printer that works by directing ink droplets onto the paper
graphics (computer):	any computer output except letters or numbers
matrix printer:	a printer using a matrix print-head
microdisk:	small disk (3½-inch standard) used in microcomputers
network:	computers and other devices linked together in such a way that they can share information and communicate with each other
output device:	anything controlled directly by a computer and used by it to provide information or action (e.g. *printer, modem,* etc.)
peripherals:	any machine connected to the computer and forming part of the system (e.g. all input and output devices)
sheet feed:	a machine for feeding individual sheets of paper into a printer one after another
tractor feed:	part of a printer enabling continuous stationery to be used

The following terms appear in Section F

bar-code:	printed code comprising stripes of various thicknesses that can be read into a computer by means of a pen-shaped *bar-code reader*
facsimile machine:	a machine which can transmit an exact copy of a document over a long distance through the use of *network*
file-locking:	the process by which a computer in a *network* prevents other users from looking at a file which is being worked on
modem:	a device that enables computers to send information down telephone lines (from MOdulator/DEModulator)
workstation:	a *terminal* or computer connected to a *network,* at which someone sits and works

D. Check your grammar

> **Remember**
> He won a million pounds and went on a world tour.
> *If* I won a million pounds, *I would* go on a world tour.

Now make up sentences on this model, using the following phrases as starters. You may start: "If I . . .", "If you . . ." etc. as you wish. Then work with another student by putting questions, to which he or she must reply.

For example: If you won a million pounds, what would you do?

Starters:
- pass my exam
- get that job
- know you were coming
- have the time
- meet the Prime Minister
- see the opportunity
- manage to find one
- show her this
- open that door
- tell him that

E. Understanding a lecture

Listen to the lecture on your tape, repeating it section by section. Make notes for answers to the following questions, then combine them into a summary of the contents of the lecture.

- What do safety regulations say about fire extinguishers?
- How does the use of computers influence smoking in offices?
- What three reasons are given for not smoking at work?
- Does use of VDUs for several hours a day have any effect on health?
- How great is the risk of radiation?
- Why do people in offices sometimes become irritable?
- What is the name of the main law on health at work?
- What points are covered in it?
- How have trade unions contributed to improving working conditions?
- Why is it still necessary to be constantly alert?
- What law was passed in 1974?
- In what two offices can employees find copies of these laws?

F. Understanding a printed text (2)

11.11 Networks

local area
wide area

Computers and other machines can be linked together so that information can be passed from one to another. Such a link-up is called a *network*. There are two forms of network, the *local area network*, and the *wide area network*. The local area network is confined to an office, or at most to a building. Wide area networks can span the world.

Networking greatly increases the power and flexibility of computers and their peripherals. Just about the simplest form of local area network would be two microcomputers sharing a Winchester disk and a printer, illustrated in Figure 11.3. Each machine works separately until it needs to access the disk. Then it uses the network to write on or read from the disk (computer terminology uses 'write' and 'read' instead of 'record' and 'play', but it means the same). If both computers tried to use the disk simultaneously there would obviously be problems, so various systems are used to ensure that every

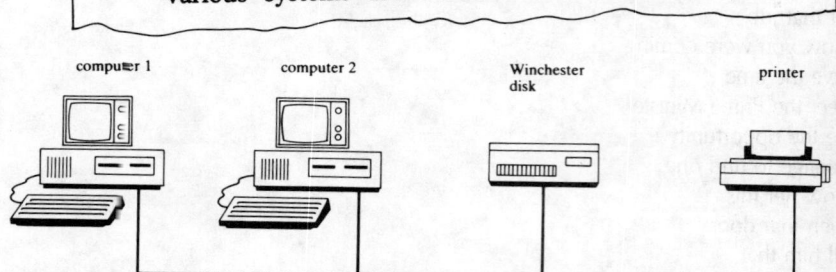

Figure 11.3 A very simple network. Not only can either computer use the Winchester disk or printer, but information can also be sent from one computer to the other.

machine on the network checks that the network is free, and if necessary waits. Because the rate at which data is transmitted through the network is very rapid, there is not usually a perceptible delay.

Other more subtle problems can arise. Suppose the first computer was in use updating an accounts file. Unknowingly, someone uses the second computer to print out the same file. The result could be wrong information on the printout, caused by the second computer working on a partially updated file. To solve this problem, a technique known as *file locking* is used. The computer carrying out the updating locks the file, so that no other machines can use it.

file locking

A more complicated network is shown in Figure 11.4. This shows a minicomputer, with a network of microcomputers, printers, and other machines, such as might be used in a modern office. Note that there is a dedicated word processor (basically a computer specially designed for word processing and unusable for other purposes), a telex machine and three types of printer. Each microcomputer or terminal that is linked to the network is referred to as a *workstation*.

As each microcomputer has access to the files held on the hard disk system of the minicomputer, information held there can be obtained by any of the microcomputers, subject to the right password. Thus the accounts manager can obtain historical data about sales, for example, and use his micro-

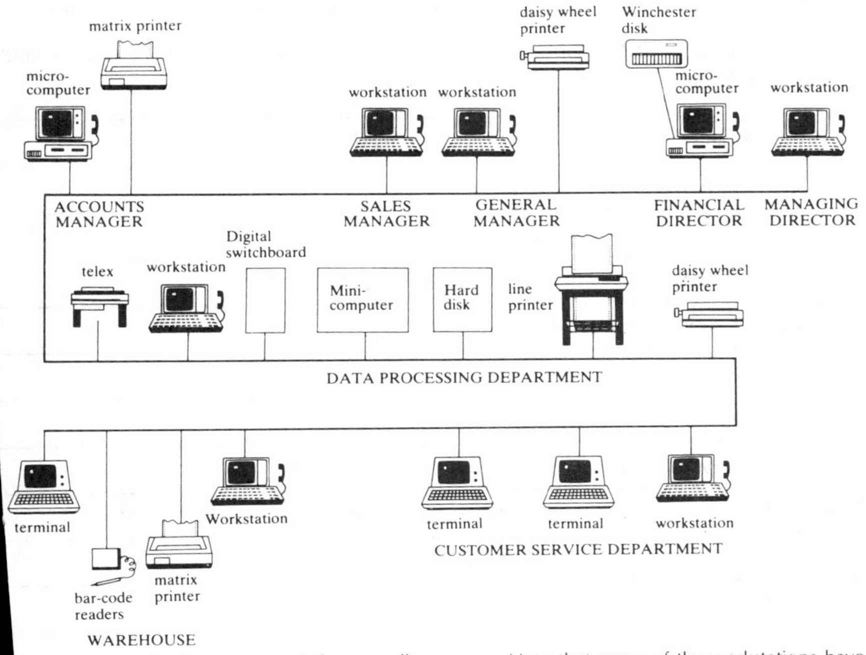

Figure 11.4 A local area network for a small company. Note that some of the workstations have telephones for an 'electronic mail' system.

computer to produce his statistics. In the illustration the accounts manager has a matrix printer; the general manager has a daisy wheel printer—why do you think this is?

Wide area networks link offices in different parts of the country—or even different parts of the world—by special communication lines. In the United Kingdom the lines are provided by British Telecom. Transatlantic and other long-distance links are usually made by satellite. Wide area networks link the same kinds of machine as local area networks, but you may well find a *facsimile machine* at each end of the long-distance link. The facsimile machine can scan any document or photograph and transmit a copy of it to the machine at the other end of the link.

It is possible to transmit information over the normal 'speech' telephone lines, using a device called a *modem*. The output of the computer is converted into an audible signal, and sent down the telephone lines. A modem at the other end translates the signal for the receiving computer. Because telephone lines are intended for speech, they are not ideal for data. The speed of transmission is only a fraction of what can be obtained using proper data lines, and the reliability is not as good. The one advantage is that of cheapness.

G. Check your understanding

Read through the text carefully, looking up anything you do not understand. Then answer the following questions:

1. What two kinds of computer networks are there?
2. What is the difference?
3. What is the advantage of networking?
4. What do the computer terms *write* and *read* mean?
5. Does it take much time for data to pass through a network?
6. What is the purpose of *file-locking*?
7. What is a *dedicated* word-processor?
8. What is a *workstation*?
9. How are offices in a network linked within an area such as one country?
10. How are long-distance links usually made?
11. What does a *facsimile* machine do?
12. What is the use of a *modem*?

H. Understanding discourse

Look at the following picture and text carefully. Then listen to your tape and answer the questions the tutor asks you.

Figure 13.3 Monarch call-connect system. (Courtesy of Merlin, British Telecom Business Systems)

For the extension user

Call diversion extension user instructs system to divert all calls to another extension if his own is engaged or does not answer.

Abbreviated dialling up to 20 numbers can be stored and retrieved in response to short code dialled by extension user.

Last number recall automatic dialling of a previously engaged number.

Call back extension is automatically connected to a previously engaged or unanswered number when that number next completes a call.

Inquiry calls extension user can hold a call while consulting another extension or number and can alternate between the two numbers or return to the held call.

Call transfer to operator if a transferred call fails the caller is not cut off as the call is automatically reconnected with the operator.

Extension group hunting extensions are grouped according to type of work handled; equipment searches for a free extension in the group when a call comes in.

Conference calls up to four parties can hold a conference, including one on an outside line.

Call barring equipment can be instructed to prevent outgoing calls or some types of outgoing call to be made from some extensions or to prevent incoming calls.

Operator paging extensions extension can be signalled to indicate that switchboard operator has a message.

Incoming call to engaged number a special tone indicates to an extension that an incoming call is waiting.

Music-while-waiting waiting caller is reassured by the sound of background music that he remains connected while the call is being attended to.

Material taken from TROTMAN, *Modern Secretarial Procedures*, McGraw-Hill, 1986

UNIT 15

THE SIX WAYS OF IMPROVING PROFITS

A. Understanding a printed text (1)

Every businessman wants to increase profits. This text tells him how! Read it quickly and answer the following questions:

1. Which of the six courses is different from all the others?
2. What can you tell from Figure 2.1?
3. Do you think all the ways of increasing profits are equally effective?

The six ways of improving profits

Fundamentally, there are only six different ways in which profits can be improved. These are:

1. Increase selling prices.
2. Increase sales volume.
3. Decrease direct costs (labour and material).
4. Decrease overhead costs.
5. Change the sales mix.
6. Buy another company.

The percentage on capital employed can be improved by disposing of unnecessary fixed or working assets, which may release cash but does not contribute directly to profits.

2.1 Increasing selling prices

Charging more for products or services seems a relatively easy way to improve results. A small price increase, say 5 per cent, can give rise to a much larger increase in profit, for example, 20 per cent. However, in some companies price can have a significant effect on the volume of sales, particularly if there is direct competition from other companies.

There are many factors which affect selling prices, and they must not be neglected in the efforts to improve profitability. Some of these are:

competitor's prices

1. The prices which competitors are charging for the same product or service.

cost structures

2. The cost structure of the business. Some costs will vary in proportion to the quantity of goods produced, e.g., bought-out materials and parts and direct labour—these are called 'variable costs'. Other costs will remain relatively constant for significant changes in the quantity of goods produced—these are called 'fixed costs'. It is important that the effects of selling price and volume on these two types of cost are fully understood and analysed before any decision on price increases is made.

3. The price elasticity of the commodity. The effect that price has on volume should be realistically assessed and calculations should be made concerning the relative profitability of varying prices and volumes. Where necessary, price–volume curves should be drawn up on graphs for differing products or product groups; the point of maximum profit for that given time can then be calculated.

price elasticity

For some products, price will affect the sales volume very sharply. This can happen in the market-place, where the same goods are displayed in the same vicinity and price is the main purchasing criteria. The goods—for instance, apples of the same size, quality, and grade—are offered immediately for sale, alongside other goods of the same characteristics.

For other products, price is not the main purchasing criterion. When buying a fur coat, the quality and species of fur, the shape of the design, its originality, the quality of fittings and linings, and even the name have far more effect on the purchaser than price. A 5 per cent increase for this commodity would probably have no effect on the volume sold at all.

There are generally three main factors which affect purchasing decisions, with other sub-factors:

(a) Design — for function or use;
— for style and shape;
— for reliability in use.

(b) Price — cost of the article;
— cost of use.

(c) Delivery — time scale—how long it takes to get the goods;
— reliability—keeping to promises made.

4. Price increases within an inflationary market situation may mean that the increases are only keeping pace with rises in costs. These increases would not improve profitability unless the percentage change was above the percentage inflation rate.

price increases

2.2 Increasing sales volume

The effect on profits of increasing sales volume can be illustrated by the use of the break-even chart (Fig. 2.1). It can be seen that, although sales volume has increased by about 25 per cent from A to B, profits have increased by about 150 per cent.

Not every company can increase sales volume by as much as 25 per cent per annum, although perhaps this should be the target. It is important that the increase in volume is on profitable goods—otherwise the overall profits will not increase.

Increases in volume can be obtained in the following ways:

By increasing market penetration of existing areas (increasing market share).

By finding new markets for existing products/services.

With an already full order book, by increasing production or removing restrictions on supplies.

Categories 1 and 2 are the result of improved marketing and selling, while 3 is usually obtained through improvements in production control or materials management; better control over quality; or productivity improvement methods, such as industrial engineering and incentive schemes.

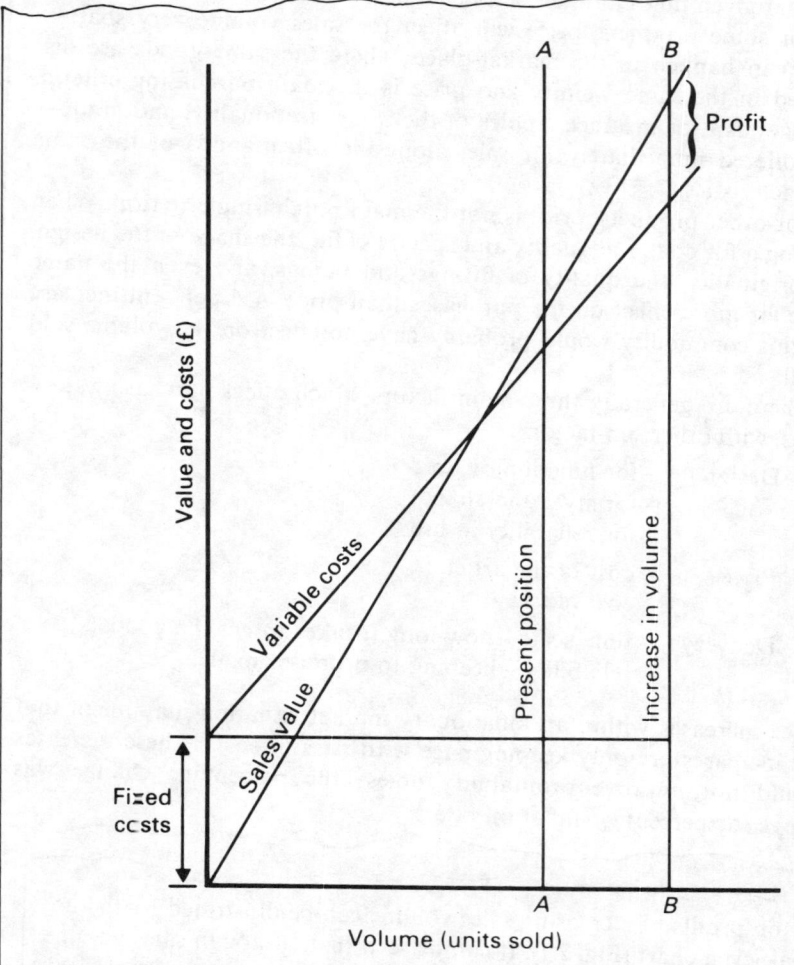

Fig. 2.1 Break-even chart showing the effect of increasing sales on profits

2.3 Decreasing direct costs

These are usually viewed as the costs which increase in proportion to volume. However, a more strict definition for direct costs would be those which can be directly attributable to a specific activity—'the costs you wouldn't incur if you didn't do it'.

Direct costs are usually costs of materials or services which form part of the actual product or service—the wages and indirect expenses of employing people who are involved in the manufacture of goods or services, and the overheads that can be directly attributable to the product or service.

Direct costs are usually allocated but not apportioned to the product or service. In many methods of costing we perform detailed calculations to apportion parts of cost recovery to products; for example, local authority rates are often apportioned by square metres to recover costs using an overhead cost rate for each department. In real life, rates will remain the same whether or not a specific product is made. They should be controlled in total, and recovered through contribution. Apportionment is merely fiddling with figures.

The benefits of decreasing direct costs are very helpful to profit improvement. For instance, a reduction of 5 per cent in materials costs can in some companies provide a 20 per cent improvement in profits. However, cost-cutting exercises that result in a decrease in value to the customer—e.g., purchasing poorer-quality materials—will not be helpful.

Ways in which costs can be reduced include:

1. Securing reductions in purchase price for the same material.
2. Improving the yield of items from the same material.
3. Reducing the number of components which make up a product, but with the same quality and performance.
4. Reducing the work content of operations and processes.
5. Reducing scrap and rectification work.

The methods for securing these reductions are:

— More effective purchasing.

— Better pre-production planning.

— Value analysis and engineering.

— Work study, industrial engineering, and manufacturing engineering.

— Quality assurance and control.

— Incentive schemes.

— Production planning and control; materials management.

2.4 Decreasing overhead costs

By definition, these costs are 'overheads'—the costs we have to recover through our contribution towards sales, which are the costs of supporting the business. Typical of such costs are:

1. Telephone.
2. Stationery.
3. Rates.
4. Electricity.
5. Water consumption.
6. Indirect salaries and employment costs for:
    - Marketing and sales.
    - Engineering, R & D.
    - Finance.
    - Administration.
    - Manufacturing services.

Excess costs can be identified and controlled for each element of costs. Take telephones, for example: here, companies will often restrict their use until after 12 noon to secure reduced rates of charge except for necessary calls. They may even log the duration of each call and note the persons making calls so that control data are available and any excesses are eliminated.

However, the largest element of costs in overheads are those of employing people. The costs of employing one person can include:

- Salary.
- Expenses (travelling, car, hotels, etc.).
- Employment costs (government charges and pension schemes).
- Telephone usage.
- Stationery usage.
- Electricity usage.

The employment of people *is* expensive, and while it may be painful to have to part with employees, it is the quickest and most effective way of reducing overheads. Needless to say, good people are important to a company, as they often possess skills and knowledge which provide expensive benefits to business operations. Reduction in 'deed and word' and ineffective administration services should be actively sought; each department must justify itself by providing financial advantages for the costs incurred.

Each element of overhead expense and activity should be investigated and controlled. The techniques to achieve this are:

1. Organization and methods.
2. Business analysis.
3. Office equipment and computerization.
4. Budgetary control.

B. Check your understanding

Read through the text carefully, looking up anything you do not understand. Then answer the following questions:

1. Does selling fixed assets increase profits?
2. What beneficial effect does it have?
3. What negative effect may an increase in sales price have?
4. Is the price charged by competitors important in fixing the price of a product?
5. What analysis should be done before decisions about price changes are made?
6. What sort of visuals could be useful in such an analysis?
7. Name three factors that may have more influence on the sales of an expensive item than just the price.
8. How does a good brand image affect the price of a product?
9. What are the three main considerations influencing a potential purchaser?
10. How might you increase your profit in a situation of five per cent annual inflation?
11. Do sales volume and profitability always increase by the same percentage?
12. What might be a reasonable target for a company to increase its annual sales volume?
13. What are the parameters of the graph in Figure 2.1?
14. In Figure 2.1, what is the projected effect of an increase in sales: (a) on fixed costs?; (b) on sales value?; (c) on variable costs?; (d) on profit:
15. How do you define direct costs?
16. What five examples of direct costs can you cite?
17. Are cost-cutting exercises always good for the customer?
18. In what way can a reduction in costs be harmful?
19. What general term is used to mean the costs of supporting a business?
20. What is the biggest item in a company's overheads?

C. Increase your vocabulary

1. Explain in your own words what the following mean, as used in the text:

- paragraph 2.1, 2 line 3: variable costs
  5: fixed costs

- paragraph, 2.1, 3 line 1: price elasticity
  3: relative profitability
  13: purchasing criterion

- paragraph 2.1, 4 line 1: inflationary market situation

- paragraph 2.2, line 2: break-even

- paragraph 2.2, 1 line 1: market penetration

- paragraph 2.2, 3 line 1: full order book

- page 144, line 4: incentive schemes

- paragraph 2.3, line 8: overheads
  15: apportionment
  lines 15–16: fiddling with figures

- paragraph 2.3, 2: yield of items
  5: rectification work

- paragraph 2.4, 6: R & D

2. What words or expressions could you use to replace the following without substantially changing the meaning?

- introduction, line 1: fundamentally
  9: disposing of

- paragraph 2.1, line 1: relatively easy way
  4: have a significant effect on
  2.1, 2, line 2: bought-out materials
  2.1, 3, line 5: the point of maximum profit
  9: in the same vicinity

- paragraph 2.3, line 8: directly attributable to
  lines 19–20: cost-cutting exercises
  line: 31: pre-production planning

- paragraph 2.4, line 9: indirect salaries
  last line: budgetary control

D. Check your grammar

> **Remember**
> She missed the bus and arrived late for the lecture.
> If she hadn't missed the bus, she wouldn't have arrived late for the lecture.

1. Now complete the following sequence:
- If she hadn't arrived late for the lecture . . . (miss the revision)
- If she hadn't missed the revision . . . (fail the test)
- If she hadn't failed the test . . . (be given extra reading)
- If she hadn't been given extra reading . . (work all night)
- If she hadn't worked all night . . . (got up so late)
- If she hadn't got up so late . . . (miss the bus)

2. Working with another student if possible, make up similar sequences on the basis of the following starters:
- If you had told me that sooner . . .
- If someone hadn't switched the power off . . .
- If we'd used the right program . . .
- If you'd been to the lecture . . .
- If she hadn't gone to that party . . .

E. Understanding a lecture

Listen to the lecture on your tape and answer these questions:
1. What is the purpose of a trade union?
2. What four benefits do all trade unions offer?
3. What other organisations are there which are similar to Trade Unions?
4. For whom are such organisations intended?
5. Do members of trade unions have to pay?
6. Is membership of a trade union obligatory?
7. Do all employers encourage their staff to join trade unions?
8. What reasons can you think of for and against joining a trade union?

F. Understanding a printed text (2)

2.5 Changing the sales mix

The advantages of concentrating on some areas of the business at the expense of others can be large. This particularly applies to product ranges. Some products will make a greater profit than others—or, more strictly, some will make a greater contribution to overheads and profits than others.

'Contribution' is defined as the difference between actual selling prices (such as catalogue prices less discount) and all direct costs. Profit is *not* made on each product, but only when enough contribution has been made to recover the overhead costs: after that point, contribution is all profit. This is important to recognize.

Getting the appropriate sales mix is very important, because one could increase total sales by 30 per cent and still make a lower profit if the wrong products are sold. Concentrating on the higher-contribution products is the answer.

The following actions would also be included in this category:

1. Concentration on higher added value products:
   - Upgrading the product on offer to give better value to the customer.
2. Adding new products and services to the existing ones offered.

The techniques useful in this category are:

1. Management accounting:
   - Contribution analysis, direct costing, profit planning.
2. Value analysis.

2.6 Buying another company

This method of improving profits is overlooked in many companies and emphasized in others. There are obvious dangers and pitfalls to be avoided; but to the well managed company there can be a lot of advantages. Take-overs, mergers, and the like are used by many groups to provide the kind of growth in company performance desired by institutional investors.

It is interesting that the balance sheet value of a company—the fixed assets plus current assets less current liabilities, or net worth of a company, as portrayed in the accounts—gives little indication of what a business is really worth. This will depend on the viewpoint of the buyer; for instance:

1. The value of a company could be equated to the potential profit earnings over a few years and the investment which would justify purchase.
2. The value of the company could be viewed as the extent of the assets owned—buildings, plant and equipment, vehicle stocks, etc. These will be viewed differently too.
   (a) If the company is ceasing to operate, the value may be only a fraction of the book value.

(b) If the company is being bought as a going concern, the realistic value of assets may be much more than the book value. For instance, building values will have increased, but book values will have reduced—purchase price less depreciation.

3. Combination of 1 and 2 above.
4. Other factors, e.g., buying out competition.

Additional profits are often gained through take-over, and often at an investment price which is well justified.

There are no specific techniques, but the following are often useful:

1. Put in good management.
2. Employ a good business 'turn-around' specialist.
3. Employ experienced and knowledgeable management consultants.
4. Appoint experienced and knowledgeable non-executive directors.

2.7 Summary

Each company will need to explore for itself which way of improving profits is likely to yield the most benefits. All six ways of profit improvement must be tackled or explored, but in most companies there are usually a few things which, if they are done effectively, will yield substantial results. Most companies are not bad at everything—otherwise they would not be in business. In most business improvement or turn-around exercises, the skill is to select what really needs improving to get results.

G. Check your understanding

Read through the passages carefully, looking up anything you do not understand. Then say whether the authors agree with the following statements or not:

- It is best to concentrate on a few areas of a business rather than giving equal attention to them all. ☐
- All products in one range should be equally profitable. ☐
- Profit does not begin until enough contribution has been made to cover overheads. ☐
- A profitable business concentrates on higher contribution products. ☐
- The net worth of a company is clearly visible from its balance sheet. ☐
- The real worth of a company is less easy to display. ☐

H. Understanding discourse

Listen to your tutor talking on your tape about basic documents showing the financial state of a company. Then look at the sample balance sheet given below and answer the tutor's questions.

WISDOM AND SOLOMON, PARTNERS

Balance Sheet as at 31 March 19

	£	£	£
Fixed assets			
Plant and machinery		21 600	
Furniture and fittings		7 640	
			29 240
Current assets			
Stock	3 600		
Sundry debtors	15 200		
Cash at bank	1 060		
Cash in hand	400		
		20 260	
Current liabilities			
Sundry creditors		12 500	
			7 760
			37 000
less Long-term loan			10 000
			27 000
Capital			
T. Wisdom			15 000
K. Solomon			12 000
			27 000

From: TROTMAN, *Modern Secretarial Procedures*, McGraw-Hill, 1986

The text of this unit was taken from PRABHU and BAKER, *Improving Business Performance*, McGraw-Hill, 1986